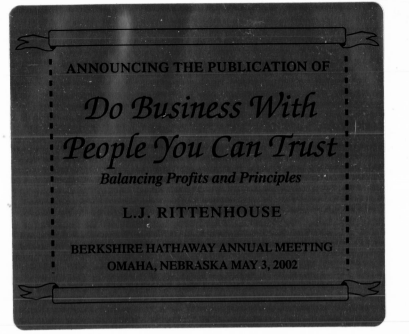

ANNOUNCING THE PUBLICATION OF

Do Business With People You Can Trust

Balancing Profits and Principles

L.J. RITTENHOUSE

BERKSHIRE HATHAWAY ANNUAL MEETING
OMAHA, NEBRASKA MAY 3, 2002

Do Business With People You Can Tru$t

Balancing Profits & Principles

Do Business With People You Can Tru$t

Balancing Profits & Principles

L.J. Rittenhouse

First Printing, May 2002

Printed in the United States of America
ISBN 0-9719356-0-2

Library of Congress Control Number: 2002105008

*To Ruth who did the work of angels
and to my daughter who, each day,
reminds me to look for angels.*

Do Business With People You Can Tru$t

Balancing Profits & Principles

Contents

Preface

My mission to critique the shareholder letters that CEOs publish in annual reports started in 1992. It grew out of a special project I did for a CEO who commissioned my company to develop his investor relations program. He shared my belief in the importance of candid and clear financial communications to ensure that his company's stock traded at a fair, not a "hyped" price.

A centerpiece of this program was working with the CEO to rethink the importance of his annual letter to shareholders. More often than not, this communication published in the company's annual report did little to advance the company's credibility or value in the marketplace. We wanted to change that perception and publish a letter with meaningful disclosure. But we needed a standard to judge what was meaningful.

A year later, after reading the extensive shareholder letter written by Warren Buffett, the Chairman and CEO of Berkshire Hathaway, I created a model to analyze the content in CEO shareholder letters. This model, **LanguageWorks** *for business*[SM], identifies and sorts the topics that are commonly found in shareholder letters. It challenges skeptics who believe that letters are highly subjective and cannot be analyzed. People use my model to systematically identify the presence or absence of these topics.

When many topics are clearly and candidly reported in a letter, readers get a highly informative communication. Conversely, when few topics are addressed and readers find more fluff than facts, they learn to dismiss CEO letters as a waste of valuable reading time. In the chapters that follow, I describe these topics and show how we correlate our shareholder letter disclosure findings with company stock prices.

When I wrote Warren Buffett about my work in 1997, he wrote back acknowledging the importance of this original research. He invited me to the 1998 Berkshire Hathaway shareholder meeting where I could "learn firsthand about the only thing longer than my letter – namely the time that Charlie and I spend answering shareholder questions."

I went to Omaha, found that Buffett sounded in public just like he did in his annual report, and subsequently, made a small investment in the Berkshire "B" shares. They trade at $1/30^{th}$ of the "A" shares. Over the years, I informed Warren of the progress of my shareholder letter research. My ambition to write a book on the subject always got sidetracked. But the Enron bankruptcy changed my priorities.

This largest bankruptcy in history has undermined public confidence in our important business institutions: accounting and legal firms; and stock brokerage and investment banking companies. Enron's alleged abuse of investor and public trust and disclosures of questionable business practices at other large and well-known companies have made everyone deeply aware of this one fact: we want to do business with people we can trust.

This book is intended for three very different audiences. First, I hope it will be read by CEOs who want to know what investors should look for when they read shareholder letters. Since the CEO's reputation is now considered to be an important factor in valuing a company's stock price, astute executives know that quality disclosure in a shareholder letter can enhance their market standing.

In the past, the financial statements and footnotes in an annual report could be relied upon as indicators of future corporate performance. In today's hyper-paced world these financial figures are less useful and reliable. Qualitative indicators are increasingly important. Investors want to know how CEOs judge the profit potential of new business opportunities, analyze competitive advantage and demonstrate awareness of key stakeholder concerns. Astute investors look for evidence of these qualities in the shareholder letter.

This book is intended, as well, for individual investors like my mother. She is intelligent and has the capacity to analyze information in a shareholder letter. When my mother got annual reports in the past, she never looked at them. Now she has a guide to help her navigate through an annual report and to uncover meaning in shareholder letters. As my research shows, this guide will help her make better-informed investment decisions. Individual investors like my mother are invited to be part of the

Shareholder Letter Scorecard project described in Chapter 15 and to grade CEOs on the quality of disclosure in their letters.

Finally, this book is intended for the owners of Berkshire Hathaway. This group does not have to be reminded about the importance of candid communication and the power of one's word. They belong to a community where the golden rule of financial partnership remains intact: do unto your investor-partner what you would have him or her do unto you. In Omaha, at least, nice guys finish first. Why? Because nice guys balance profits and principles.

Cynics who learn about my model will say, "Ha, when CEOs figure out your formula, they'll just follow it to get a high score." They forget what most Berkshire Hathaway investors know: Warren Buffett's letters are read, studied and quoted because he discloses information that is personal, not formulaic. When you combine balanced and reliable information with principled reporting, you get a truthful and authentic communication.

Last summer, my eight-year-old daughter and I visited Warren Buffett at his Omaha office. After greeting us, he promptly took my daughter to the office copy machine and photocopied her hand. He offered the paper image to her saying, "Keep this. No one else in the world has a handprint like that." Similarly, when you read a shareholder letter, look for the CEO's unique handprint. If find this, you've found someone who can merit your trust.

Acknowledgments

I want to thank Warren Buffett for his support. This book would not have been possible without his permission to let me quote extensively from Berkshire Hathaway's copyrighted letters. Respecting his wish, I have not quoted any letters in their entirety.

When I first wrote to Warren Buffett in 1997 about my work to analyze CEO letters, he promptly he wrote back noting, "You are on the side of the angels in your mission for better writing in shareholder letters." Over the years, he continued to show interest and to encourage the development of my CEO language model. He generously set aside time to talk with me in connection with this book. The first interview was conducted in June 2001 when we discussed the topic: Do CEOs Write Their Own Shareholder Letters? The second occurred after the September 11th attacks. This time we discussed the importance of business morality.

Except for reading the transcript of our interview, he has not reviewed, nor asked to review the material prior to the book's publication. Throughout the past five years, his affirmation steadied me when others challenged my purpose.

Jack Welch, the former Chairman and CEO of General Electric, also recognized the importance of this analytic approach and offered ongoing encouragement. In a telephone interview shortly before he retired, we talked about the importance of shareholder letters for investors and, also, for the company's employees. I am grateful to both men for their belief in the value of this research.

I would also like to thank Debbie Bosanek, Mr. Buffett's assistant, who efficiently responded to my requests for information and advice. I've enjoyed swapping stories with her about our children. I am grateful to Kelly Muchemore, also of Berkshire Hathaway, who helped to organize the launch of this book, scheduled on May 3, 2002 at the Bookworm Bookstore in Omaha. This event is part of the Berkshire Hathaway annual shareholder meeting and I am delighted to be a participant in the 2002 Capitalist Caper.

Over the years, many people, including my clients have helped to develop my **LanguageWorks** *for business*^{SM} model. In the early days these included Thomas Capps, Bill Hall, Fred Wood, Mark Lazenby, Joy Morris, Carole Hyatt, Robert Marritz, Ken McCready, Harry Schaefer, Larry Downes, Lori Backer, John Rowe, Linn Draper, Henry Fayne, Armando Pena, Betty Jo Rozsa, David Hagelin, James Pignatelli, Ira Adler, Kevin Larson, Durga Waite, Victoria Jedicke, and especially, Tom Newberry and Richard Sonstelie. More recently, this list includes Steve Snyder, Ian Bourne, Dawn Farrell, Dan Pigeon, Bill Mahoney, Richard Priory, Roberta Bowman, Sue Becht, Joe Magliochetti, Greg Smietanski, and Todd Romain.

The effort to create and produce this book has been nothing short of miraculous. I have been inordinately blessed with the opportunity to work with a team that included: Betty Robbins, Moses Silverman, Mark Lazenby, Ray Morris, John Baker, John Olson, Caren Byrd, Audree Rittenhouse, Karl Wilder, David Dowd, Rich DiSilvio, Michelle Gluckow, Carl Marucci and Ellis Levine. In particular, Peter Morris and Kathleen Cox provided invaluable on-going editorial guidance.

But this book could never have been possible without the dedication and hard work of Stephen Dandrow who has nurtured the development of the language model since its inception. The influence of his critical comments, editorial contributions, and the long hours of research to ensure the accuracy of our findings are evident throughout this book. To Stephen and to the book team, I extend my deepest gratitude.

Do Business with People You Can Trust

Balancing Profits and Principles

An Invitation

This book is written for people who want to do business with people they can trust. In business, the buck stops at the top. That's why I focus on the words of CEOs to look for trustworthy leadership. After twenty years of working with CEOs and analyzing their communications, first as an investment banker and then as an investor relations adviser, I've learned that what they say and don't say matters a great deal. It matters to the company's employees, to its partners, and especially to the investment community. It's a key factor in valuing a company's stock price. When a CEO's words are backed up by actions, his or her promises become currency that investors can take to the bank. If not, their words become as worthless as counterfeit bills.

In a post 9/11 and Enron world, this book focuses on business values and why they ought to matter to both CEOs and investors. It invites you to consider investing as entering into a partnership, not buying a lottery ticket. It breaks new ground by exploring an untapped resource: the letters that CEOs write in their annual reports. It offers the lessons learned from analyzing the granddaddy of all shareholder letters, those written by world-class investor Warren Buffett, Chairman and CEO of Berkshire Hathaway.

Buffett's remarkably candid and lengthy letters not only tell investors about the state of his company, they reveal his common sense, his decency and his business principles and practices. Yet, many people read Buffett's letter not caring a hoot about his values or principles. They're looking for investment tips. His genius for allocating capital and racking up double-digit investment returns over 30 years has earned him the title, "The Sage of Omaha."

Like his outstanding investment record, the letters he writes each year consistently outrank all other CEO letters in my annual survey. He takes pride in these annual updates. In his year 2000 shareholder letter, Buffett revealed the formula he uses for valuing investments.

Developed by a very smart man named Aesop, this time-tested principle is over 2,600 years old and known as "a bird in the hand is worth two in the bush." Good investments are made, Buffett wrote, when you ask three questions: "How certain are you that there are indeed birds in the bush? When will they emerge and how many will there be? And what is the risk-free interest rate? Answer these questions and you will know the maximum value of the bush – and the maximum number of birds you now possess that should be offered for it." He invites the literal-minded to substitute "dollars" for "birds." Likewise, readers of this book should replace "bush" with "CEO and company."

You can use this book to identify trustworthy leaders in the way that bird watchers have guides to help them identify different kinds of birds. This analogy occurred to me because of walks I took in New York's Central Park. I'd ramble over paths looking for robins, sparrows, and starlings. By the lake, I'd find ducks and, if lucky, a blue heron. These sightings rarely required binoculars. But when I visited these same places with Starr Sapphire, the city's crack Audubon ornithologist, I'd see 60 or more species of birds – from spotted woodpeckers to yellow-bellied sapsuckers. Why? She showed me where to point my binoculars and what to look for.

Consider me the Starr Sapphire of CEO language. Let this guide show you how to spot CEO language that you can trust. If you study it carefully, it will help you to identify the kinds of bushes that may be hiding the most promising birds.

Happy hunting!

Chapter One

Do Business with People You Can Trust:
A Post 9/11 Commandment

Avoid business involving moral risk: No matter what the rate, you can't write good contracts with bad people. While most policyholders and clients are honorable and ethical, doing business with the few exceptions is usually expensive.
Berkshire Hathaway Inc., Third Quarter Letter to Shareholders
November 9, 2001

Trust is a feeling and an action. Trust is a choice. If we want to be deemed trustworthy, we must trust others. When we trust someone, we feel safe with that person and lower our defenses. In a post 9/11 and post Enron world, trust seems to be in increasingly short supply. Investors who seek to find someone or something to trust need look no further than the heartland of America, specifically Omaha, Nebraska.

This state capital is home to the world headquarters of Berkshire Hathaway Inc. and its Chairman and CEO, Warren Buffett. If you had trusted him to invest $10,000 of your money in 1965 when he took control of Berkshire Hathaway, your investment would be worth over $50 million by 2002. Conversely, if you had invested the same amount of money in the S&P 500 index, it would have grown to $500,000, only 1 percent of Berkshire's return.[1] This extraordinary CEO has created a small community of billionaires. And since he has never sold any of his shares, his personal stake in Berkshire is nearly $35 billion.

I became acquainted with Buffett seven years ago when his stock was trading at about $25,000 a share. Someone gave me his shareholder letter to read. It was not like other CEO letters. His letter was candid, informative and educational. It even made me laugh. It spurred me on to create a model to measure the effectiveness of CEO letters by comparing leadership language and stock price performance. I call it **LanguageWorks** *for business*[SM].

Every year when I read Buffett's letters, I find new topics to add to the shareholder letter model.

Reading his quarterly shareholder letter published after the September 11th attacks was a case in point. In this communication, Buffett reminded investors of his three rules for running a successful insurance business. The first two rules involve the careful analysis and pricing of insured risks. His third rule was surprising. It advised readers to avoid moral risk by doing business with good people.

This was a new Buffett commandment. He wrote the important words of advice that I placed at the head of this chapter: "No matter what the rate, you can't write good contracts with bad people. While most policyholders are honorable and ethical, doing business with the few exceptions is usually expensive."

When I interviewed Buffett to talk about this letter, morality was clearly on his mind. He told me that it's not possible to make a good deal with bad people. He used a powerful analogy to illustrate his new commandment, "Doing business with people who cause your stomach to churn is like marrying for money: it's a bad idea and it's particularly crazy if you're already rich."[2]

Rebuilding Trust

To many people, business morality sounds like an oxymoron. My minister says that I am the first person he has ever met to suggest that business people could be moral. Preaching in the shadow of the Empire State Building, he knew many of the firemen from a nearby station who responded to the alarm on September 11th and never came back. Now, in the wake of those pivotal events, a lot of people say that they no longer feel safe.

The disintegrating fortunes of Enron and Arthur Andersen have further shaken our sense of financial security. These companies show what happens when business people forget that reputations are based on words and actions, and cannot be bought. Like the buildings that were leveled in the attacks, our ability to trust business leaders must be rebuilt from the ground up.

The managers of companies that Buffett likes to acquire share certain common characteristics. They exemplify trust-inspiring behavior. This paragraph from his 2000 shareholder letter ranks high in my research for showing how moral values are integral to Berkshire's plans to create investor wealth:

We like to do business with someone who loves his company, not just the money that a sale will bring him (though we certainly understand why he likes that as well). When this emotional attachment exists, it signals that important qualities will likely be found within the business: honest accounting, pride of product, respect for customers, and a loyal group of associates having a strong sense of direction. The reverse is apt to be true, also. When an owner auctions off his business, exhibiting a total lack of interest in what follows, you will frequently find that it has been dressed up for sale, particularly when the seller is a "financial owner." And if owners behave with little regard for their business and its people, their conduct will often contaminate attitudes and practices throughout the company.

Behavior That Destroys Trust

Buffett's 2000 letter also described behavior that destroys trust. He and Berkshire's Vice-Chairman, Charlie Munger, challenged CEOs who predict their companies will grow at high double-digit rates in the face of evidence that shows few have ever done so. But it's not the lofty predictions that anger Buffett, it's the accounting shenanigans and business compromises that accompany them. Try to find another CEO who compares questionable accounting practices to getting held up at gunpoint:

The problem arising from lofty predictions [of earnings per-share growth rates] *is not just that they spread unwarranted optimism. Even more troublesome is the fact that they corrode CEO behavior. Over the years, Charlie and I have observed many instances in which CEOs engaged in uneconomic operating maneuvers so that they could meet earnings targets they had announced. Worse still, after exhausting all that operating acrobatics would do, they sometimes played a wide variety of accounting games to "make the numbers." These accounting shenanigans have a way of snowballing: Once a company moves earnings from one period to another, operating shortfalls that occur thereafter require it to engage in further accounting maneuvers that must be even more "heroic." These can turn fudging into fraud. (More money, it has been noted, has been stolen with the point of a pen than at the point of a gun.)*

Remember, Buffett wrote this when cracks in the great 15-year bull market were just beginning to show. Dot.com stocks were falling and cash was coming back in favor as a source of investor confidence. The bankruptcies of Enron and Global Crossing were still in the future. When these giants began to crumble, it became clear that value-destroying accounting practices had spread from start-ups to companies with pedigrees.

Buffett's 2001 shareholder letter continued to shine light on the shameful behavior of CEOs. When I asked him in an interview if his criticisms of unethical CEO behavior were making him less popular on the corporate golf circuit, Buffett laughed and replied, "I'm like the Salvation Army, I hate the sin and love the sinner. I don't name names."[3] He doesn't need to add the names in the situation described below. Most people know how to fill in the blanks when he discusses:

> ... *the situation, so common in the last few years, in which shareholders have suffered billions in losses while the CEOs, promoters, and other higher-ups who fathered these disasters have walked away with extraordinary wealth. Indeed, many of these people were urging investors to buy shares while concurrently dumping their own, sometimes using methods that hid their actions. To their shame, these business leaders view shareholders as patsies, not partners.*

Living Your Principles

Buffett knows that talk can be cheap. Honesty and integrity are words that build trust only when they are backed by actions. Buffett's father, Howard, set a great example. When Buffett Senior was elected to the U.S. Congress from Omaha in 1943, the House of Representatives voted to raise their salaries from $10,000 to $12,500. Howard turned back the $2,500 raise. The increase wasn't part of the agreement that he had struck with his voters.[4]

In our interview, Warren Buffett reflected, "Living your principles doesn't cost you anything in the end. I've told students that I'm not 100 percent sure that honesty is the only policy that works. But it *does* work and it leaves you happy while it works.

Not only are you able to sleep better at night, but you get to look your kids in the eye."

The Golden Rule of Financial Partnership

Buffett gets angry when he sees behavior that violates the golden rule of financial partnership: do unto your partner what you would have him or her do unto you. When he buys a sizeable investment position in a company, he imagines himself a partner and expects to be treated like one.

His views on investor-partners are unlike those of any other CEO. He strives to keep investor turnover low. Investment professionals who make money from trading don't get rich trading Berkshire stock. He thinks of Berkshire's investors as customers who come back regularly to dine at a restaurant where they know they will get great food and reliable service. Good CEOs follow this example. If Buffett's letters sound folksy and family-like, it's because he considers investors as part of his financial family. And Buffett has actually known many of his investors much of his lifetime.

The price of owning one Class A share of Berkshire Hathaway was over $70,000 at the time this book was published. This compares to the average $42 share price on the New York Stock Exchange.[5] The high price of admission solidifies his investor base. Not many folks can ante up the cash required to join the Berkshire club. But if you do join, you receive an Owner's Manual along with your stock certificate. This manual, written in 1983, covers the principles that guide Buffett and Charlie Munger in managing the company.

The manual lays out the operating rules of the company so investors know what they can expect from management. When I tell my corporate clients about the Berkshire Hathaway Owner's Manual, they love the idea and say that they will write one for their own company. It seldom gets done.

Buffett doesn't expect other companies to produce Owner's Manuals. "Why should they?" he asks. "They wouldn't make any more money from doing it." But then, why do he and Charlie Munger do it? He says it's because he and Charlie inherited "fiduciary genes." Buffett laughs when he says, "We didn't get the Mother Teresa gene."[6] Instead, they got a fiduciary gene that drives them to inspire trust in their business. It is part of their DNA. (In their case, DNA stands for *Do the Numbers Accurately*.) It is their nature to treat the shareholders of Berkshire Hathaway as their partners.

Making Money *With* and *Not Off* Shareholders

As investor-partners, Buffett and Munger choose to make money *with* and *not off* shareholders. This is obviously not a post Enron decision, but a long-standing hallmark of Buffett's principles and philosophy.

In fact, Buffett is a virtual Scrooge when it comes to spending shareholder money. He pays himself only $100,000 a year, which is a pittance compared to most other CEOs.[7] He neither gets nor gives away stock options, a practice he abhors because it inflates earnings and dilutes the value of the company for existing shareholders. He proudly writes in his letter that the global headquarters of his $100 billion corporate empire has only 13.8 employees. (The .8 is a part-time accountant.)[8] As a result, they all wear many hats from Chief Financial Officer to the Annual Shareholder Meeting Movie Producer.

Both Buffett and Munger are highly critical of the exorbitant compensation paid to CEOs. They believe that these packages not only fail to motivate, but they can corrode CEO behavior. Munger unabashedly shared his views on this subject at a recent Berkshire Hathaway Annual Meeting:

> *I do think it will have pernicious effects on the country in its entirety as management pay keeps escalating because I think you're getting a widespread perception that the very top corporate salaries in America are obscene. And it is not a good thing for a civilization when the leaders are regarded as not dealing fairly with those for whom they are stewards.*
>
> *As for the compensation consultants who advise them on those salaries – well, all I can say is that for them, prostitution would be a step up.*[9]

The widening gap between CEO compensation and the rest of us undermines our belief in fair play. Without this reasonable expectation, people are more likely to skirt the rules rather than to play by them. A report issued in 2001 confirmed that in the 1990s, CEO pay increased 571 percent while the pay of average workers increased only 37 percent.[10]

Here are the numbers presented in historic context: "In 1960, the average CEO made twice the $100,000 salary paid to President Kennedy. In 1970, the average CEO made three times the pay of President Nixon. In 2001, the average CEO made 31 times President Bush's salary, even after it was doubled to $400,000."[11]

Every year *BusinessWeek* publishes an annual survey that compares CEO compensation with the returns that these CEOs produce for investors. The survey often shows an inverse relationship: CEOs who receive more modest compensations actually do better for their shareholders. Buffett consistently ranks at the top of the list of CEOs who provide their investors with the highest returns for the least compensation.

Buffett shuns corporate privilege. Not long ago, a partner in an important New York money management firm sat next to Buffett at a large fund-raising dinner. After the last course, Buffett bid everyone goodnight and slipped out of the room. The money manager went to wait in a long line outside the hotel for his car and driver to pull up through the traffic. Thinking Buffett must have been spirited away in a limousine, he was startled to see the multibillionaire breeze by the line, hail a yellow cab and speed off down Fifth Avenue.

The Morality of Partner-Friendly Communication

Buffett expects CEOs to report clearly and candidly to their partners. When sizing up companies in which to invest, he gets a company's annual report as a first step. He ignores the photos and the footnotes and turns straight to the CEO letter.

Buffett looks to see if it reads like something written by a public relations firm or an owner-partner who talks frankly and honestly about the business. "If they're talking to me as a partner would," he told me, "that's a significant plus. If they aren't, it's a significant minus." And that's not just because they're signing their name to something they didn't author.

Says Buffett, "They may not know their business very well. Plenty of CEOs don't understand their business as well as a lot of people outside their business or even the people who work for them. They don't want to be seen as they really are. It would be like a guy talking about golf, but never playing, and saying how great a golfer he was, or having somebody else go around saying how great he is." In the end, says Buffett, " If CEOs don't talk to me directly, I'm suspect. Why should I give them my money?"[12]

My company has followed Buffett's practice of relying on CEO language and reputation, as have professional investors. These pros estimate that investor perceptions of non-financial factors, including management credibility, account for between 30 and 40 percent of a company's stock price.[13] In a fast-changing world, vital leadership qualities – the ability to motivate, inspire, and learn from mistakes, as well as the capacity to see clearly, make judgments and be decisive with limited information – are all critical to success. The language in the CEO letter indicates the presence or absence of these qualities.

Buffett knows that a CEO becomes accountable when he writes clearly about what he's done and intends to do. Buffett says, "Knowing that a good reporter is going to report on you may inspire you to do a little bit better. When writing a shareholder letter, that good reporter should be the CEO himself." [14]

A good CEO knows the importance of delivering what he promises. It's as old-fashioned as acting as if our word is our bond. When people are confident that they can rely on what we say, we win their trust.

Looking for the trust-inspiring words of CEOs is the subject of this book.

Chapter Two

If I Only Had A Brain:

Annual Fluff or Annual Report?

INTELLIGENCE. *Etymology: Middle English, from Middle French, from Latin intelligentia, from intelligent-, intelligens intelligent. Date: 14th century*

1. *the ability to learn or understand or to deal with new or trying situations: reason; also: the skilled use of reason*
2. *the ability to apply knowledge to manipulate one's environment or to think abstractly as measured by objective criteria*

      (American Heritage College Dictionary, Third Edition)

When journalists learn that I search for meaning in CEO shareholder letters, they laugh, "They're not worth the paper they're written on." Or worse, they call these letters a bunch of lies. While interviewing me on CNN, anchor Daryn Kagan confessed that she threw out stacks of unread annual reports each spring. She asked, "Why bother reading them?"[1]

When I tell individual investors how important it is to read shareholder letters, they groan. Many can't even understand what the CEO is trying to say. This fact alone, however, gives them an important insight into deciding how much to trust the company leadership. If they can't understand the letter, I question whether they would ever understand, or even trust the financial statements. I tell them to look in the shareholder letter for clues about the company's underlying motivation.

If the CEO's primary goal is to sell, rather than to educate, investors should expect to find more fluff than facts. Warren Buffett frequently rails against the practice of loading up annual reports with glossy photos and puff prose. Under Buffett's leadership, Berkshire Hathaway has always published photo-free reports. In an interview in June 2001, he complained to me, "The name of the document is 'Annual Report.' It's not the annual sales promotion piece or the annual puff piece. It's not a picture book about the company. It's the annual report. And that's what it's supposed to be, a report." [2]

So what's the beef, you might ask. Is Buffett being a tad unreasonable? All companies sell themselves. Puffing up a company's results is a time-honored tradition. But when puffery misleads investors into believing something important that is untrue, it is no longer harmless. The money investors can lose is all too real.

I've been tracking corporate fluff in annual report letters for seven years. Three years ago, in my annual survey of CEO letters, I began to compare the quality of CEO language in a shareholder letter with the company's stock price performance. I found that credible, informative and engaging letters were correlated with stronger stock prices. Conversely, letters that had more fluff and fewer facts were correlated with lower stock prices. In fact, the group of stocks in the top 15 percent of the survey, not only outperformed the bottom 15 percent, but they have consistently outperformed the S&P 500. [3]

Information or Infomercial?

It makes sense. Investors ought to sleep better knowing they own companies led by CEOs who choose candid disclosure over puffery. But how can an individual investor determine the difference? Buffett says it's not difficult. He told me, "It's like the Supreme Court said about pornography. You know it when you see it." [4]

When people complain that they can't tell the difference, I remind them of the Scarecrow in *The Wizard of Oz*. He spent the entire film searching for a brain, only to discover at the end that all he lacked was confidence to use what he had. Many investors are like the Scarecrow. They just need to use their common sense and power to discern. Here's my advice:

1. **Trust your instincts.** No matter what others might say, if you see that the Emperor is not wearing any clothes, he's naked. If the letter sounds like nonsense, it probably is.

2. **Read the lines and in between the lines.** Look to see how the CEO balances the company's profit-making ability

with its principles. Look for clarity and consistency in how they describe their financial results.

3. **Kick the tires.** If a letter seems credible, it's important to check out the CEO's claims in the real world. This will make you a more successful investor.

Trust Your Instincts

I recommend that investors first browse the annual report to see if they're getting information or an infomercial. There's a good reason why most CEO letters seem unintelligible. Often, they are riddled with jargon and glossy prose that make sense only to insiders. People outside the company end up lost in corporate fog. It can be as dense as clouds over San Francisco Bay. Here's an example from my survey of 2000 CEO letters:

> *The supply and demand fundamentals of the commodities we produce generated excellent price levels. In addition, we completed an extensive initiative that spanned the last three years, to objectively evaluate our entire asset base and existing growth opportunities. Through this process, we developed a very clear understanding of the unique value creation opportunities and financial return potential within each of our major asset areas and reaffirmed our value creation philosophy.* [5]

This company may have "a very clear understanding," but I don't. When I see writing like this, I have to believe that the CEO signed his or her name without carefully reading the letter. By signing off on fluff, the CEO shows investors a willingness to tolerate confusion over clarity. You wonder if this is how the CEO expects the company's managers to communicate.

For the past five years, I have analyzed *Fortune 500* company letters. Only one-third of the letters I surveyed are clear, candid, informative and engaging. Most of the remainder read as if written by corporate committees or public relations firms without benefit of an objective editor. The perils of group thinking and writing are painfully obvious as evidenced by letters full of jargon and clichés.

In 1999, I surveyed 59 corporate communications and investor relations officers from 52 *Fortune 500* companies. All were directly or indirectly responsible for producing the CEO letter. I wanted to understand their creative process; to find out whether they thought the letter was important; and to learn if they were satisfied with the finished product. Three key findings emerged:

→ Forty-two percent of the respondents felt that the CEO's input was insufficient to prepare the letter, particularly at the beginning of the process.

→ Seventy-seven percent of the respondents used outside input, primarily accountants and lawyers. Boards of directors were the least frequently consulted.

→ Ninety-four percent of the respondents believed the CEO letter was the most important corporate communication, but only half felt their executives shared this same view.[6]

Clichés and Technical Jargon

Without guidance from the top, it is no wonder that shareholder letters are often blanketed in fog. Sometimes lawyers and communications consultants are paid to keep readers fogged in. The unfortunate outcome of cautious and slick communication is that investors are left thinking the CEO doesn't understand her business or doesn't want others to understand it.

Fog is not necessarily intentional. Insiders at any corporation are prone to communicating this way. Corporate writers forget that this language is foreign to people outside the company and publish letters incomprehensible to general readers.

Jargon, clichés and similar roadblocks to understanding a company are easy to spot and deadly to read. More often than not, people tell me they don't read shareholder letters because they are too jargon-ridden. The following linguistic anesthesia is from the 2000 Enron shareholder letter:

> *Our talented people, global presence, financial strength and massive market knowledge have created our sustainable and unique businesses. EnronOnline will accelerate their growth. We plan to leverage all of these competitive advantages to create significant value for our shareholders.*

In a single paragraph, the letter introduces six of the most popular CEO letter clichés:

Talented people
Global presence
Market knowledge
Financial strength
Leverage competitive advantages
Create significant value for our shareholders

These are all important concepts. But so many generalities and so few specifics quickly become meaningless to any reader. Not only do such clichés fail to inspire trust, they should cause a prudent investor to wonder if the company has something to hide.

Here's my advice. When an annual report arrives in the mail, go directly to the CEO letter. Take out a red pencil and circle clichés like "to create shareholder value," and other words that don't make sense or add to your understanding of the business. When you are finished, look at the page. If you see more red than black, consider yourself warned. At this point, Warren Buffett says he would generally stop digging into a company. It's as if he is saying, how can you be comfortable with the numbers if you're not comfortable with the words?

Reading for Profits and Principles

If a shareholder letter passes the circle test for fog, read it again. This time read and underline what makes sense to you. Some shareholder letters are well-written and informative; they reveal a good deal about a company. Read in between the lines to determine how much effort the CEO is making to educate you about his or her business. Particularly look for insights about how the company balances its profits and principles. This one factor distinguishes the letters written by CEOs who score high in my survey from the poor performers.

A CEO signals his or her profit focus by reporting on the company's business opportunities and explaining how investors will benefit from them. Statements about strong credit ratings, focused market intelligence, and a keen understanding of its competitive advantage will reveal how well a company can execute its strategy. You will have gained valuable insights into the company's goals and how well-equipped it is to meet them.

Principles are equally important. A CEO builds trust when he or she reports on successes and failures; and how the latter will be addressed. Detailed statements about the values of the business and how these are practiced build trust. I also look for comments that reveal how the CEO articulates the needs of employees, customers, and investors. Does the CEO show how the company is meeting the needs of these corporate stakeholders?

CEO Gordon Bethune, who has led a remarkable turnaround at Continental Airlines, writes a letter that combines both profits and principles. Here's what he said in 2000 about the ethic of everyone winning together:

We only win when we all win together — employees, customers and stockholders.

That approach has been responsible for our record six straight years of profitability and success. We've put our trust and confidence in each other and it has paid us all huge dividends. We continue to grow the gap between ourselves and our competitors on key metrics for financial performance, customer satisfaction and employee relations.

Our employees have created a culture and atmosphere of dignity and respect for one another. That foundation has put us among Fortune magazine's "100 Best Companies to Work For in America" for the past three years. No other airline, save Southwest Airlines, has ever achieved such long-term recognition.

For our customers, that meant six straight years of award winning customer service – no other airline has ever achieved this consistently high degree of customer satisfaction and public recognition of operational excellence. J.D. Power has awarded us the top customer satisfaction award four of the past five years. This year we won both long-haul and short-haul categories, shutting out the competition entirely.

Our stockholders have reaped the rewards of our collective approach to winning with 23 consecutive profitable quarters and six straight years of profitable performance. We've used our earnings to repurchase millions of our shares, thereby increasing the earnings of the remaining shares.

We know that by ensuring that our employees, customers and stockholders all win or lose together, we can continue to maintain success for each of us.

What about letters that don't reveal the company's profits and principles?

Enron's CEO Letters

It was easy to admire Enron's transformation from a regulated natural gas transmission company into a hard-charging energy trading company. Almost single-handedly, it created a new national market in trading electricity, natural gas and other energy commodities.

But the company didn't provide much to admire in terms of disclosure in its shareholder letters. Over the past five years, it was virtually impossible to learn how Enron made its profits. It was also impossible to understand the principles that guided Enron's business. At the end of 2001 when Enron saw its stock fall from $80 to 60 cents a share, most people were shocked. I was not. Enron's shareholder letters never met the Buffett standards of clear and candid reporting. There was never a consistent voice.

As I will show in the next chapter, each year it seemed that management brought in a new public relations firm to write the shareholder letter. By 1999, I had concluded that if the Surgeon General regulated Enron, its stock would have carried this warning: "Purchased in large amounts, this investment could be harmful to your financial health." This gap between the widely held perception of the excellence of Enron's leadership and its poor execution in communicating to investors should have raised concerns.

Kick the Tires: Due Diligence

This leads us to the third step in the analysis of shareholder letters. If you've developed a positive opinion about a company after sorting out the fluff and reading for profits and principles, then it's time to conduct due diligence. You should kick the "company's tires" to see if there is tangible evidence to support the promises it has made.

Continental Airline's CEO Gordon Bethune knows the importance of keeping promises. I've discovered this by conducting my own due diligence. I talk with people who fly Continental and also to employees. When calling for travel arrangements, I pay attention to how quickly and professionally the company's agents answer my questions.

After reading Continental's CEO letter five years ago, I began choosing them over other airlines. Bethune's prose indicated that this airline cared about people. I saw this in action when I talked with flight attendants and experienced their attentive customer service. One incident particularly impressed me. When exiting a Continental plane several years ago, I was unable to find my daughter's stroller at the jet way. Who helped me? The pilot.

Not long after the September 11th attacks, I flew Continental and asked the flight attendant how CEO Gordon Bethune was holding up in the resulting turmoil. She said, "I just sent him an e-mail to tell him how things were going. I think we're going to be o.k." Surprised, I asked if he had responded. "Usually he gets back to any of us within 24 hours," she replied. "I wanted him to know that he had my support." I got similar responses from Continental's ticket agents and pilots.

I started doing due diligence on Berkshire Hathaway in 1998 when I attended the annual shareholder meeting in Omaha. At 6:00 a.m. outside the Aksarben Coliseum, I waited for the doors to open in a line with Charlie Munger's kids so we could grab good seats for the meeting. When Buffett preaches about equal treatment for all investors, this extends even to the Vice Chairman's kids.

Due Diligence that Disappoints

I had a different kind of due diligence experience when I read First Union Corporation's shareholder letter. While I was conducting a shareholder letter disclosure seminar several years ago, an investor scowled as I extolled the virtues of First Union's letter. Finally, he stood up and declared, "First Union is my bank and this is what I think about their promises." He took out his First Union Bank Card, threw it on the floor and stepped on it. This was a surprising reaction to a company that boasted about its customer service in its shareholder letters. This experience raised questions about the company's performance subsequently confirmed in media reports. In other company's performance was not lining up with its pro. company provides exemplary disclosure in the shareho and doesn't back up their talk with consistent actions, should proceed with caution.

How did investors fare who purchased Continental's stock? Over a three-year period, from to 1998 to 2001, Continental's stock gained six percent. This was particularly impressive when compared to the 56 percent decline posted by an index of airline companies. First Union's stock, on the other hand, did not match this performance. In the same three-year period leading up to its merger with the Wachovia Corporation on September 1, 2001, First Union's stock dropped 29 percent.

In other words, when CEOs create expectations and do not align these with consistent actions, they will disappoint investors and undermine their market credibility. That's why I advise CEOs *never* to write anything they cannot back up.

Trust-blazing Topics

Over the years, I've identified over one hundred different topics and subtopics that can be found in a shareholder letter. I call these topics trust-blazers. They guide me to see if the letter merits my trust. Since it's hard to remember so many topics, I've organized them into five categories that form the skeleton of all shareholder letters:

→ **Accountability** – evidence that a company delivers on its promises;

→ **Vision** – the power of a CEO's imagination, intuition and values;

→ **Strategy** – plans and actions to grow company revenues and profits;

→ **Stakeholders** – understanding customer, employee and investors needs and the commitment to meet them;

→ **Candor** – balanced and detailed disclosure that shows a company merits trust.

In the next 12 chapters, I will introduce you to the most important topics found within each of these categories. These form the core of my **LanguageWorks** *for business*[SM] model. I created this model to identify and analyze elements of excellent disclosure in CEO shareholder letters. Each topic will further prepare you to judge how much of your trust and, perhaps, your investment dollars, you should be willing to place with a CEO.

As you study each chapter, remember the Scarecrow. At the end of film, *The Wizard of Oz* didn't give him a brain. Instead he told the Scarecrow something very important. "Why, anybody can have a brain. That's a very mediocre commodity. Back where I come from, we have universities, seats of great learning, where men go to become great thinkers. And when they come out, they think deep thoughts and with no more brains than you have. But they have one thing you haven't got: a diploma."[7]

After reading this book, you will have the equivalent of an advanced degree in CEO Linguistics. As you read CEO letters and look for these topics, your vision will expand. You will be able to understand what you see, not just see what you understand. You will be able to critique a letter and extract more meaning in less time.

But you have to do the work. In the next chapter you'll learn about the first **LanguageWorks** *for business*[SM] topic: the kind of the relationship CEOs want to have with investors.

Chapter Three

One-Night Stand or Long-Term Relationship:
Dear Shareholder

RESPECT. *Etymology: Middle English, from Latin respectus, [literally, act of looking back], from respicere [to look back], regard, from re-+specere [to look]. Date: 14th century*
1. *a relation or reference to a particular thing or situation*
2. *an act of giving particular attention : consideration*
3. *high or special regard*
> *(American Heritage College Dictionary, Third Edition)*

A CEO's attitudes toward shareholders can reveal how he or she runs the business – for long-term profits or short-term gain. I read between the lines of shareholder letters to try to figure out what kind of **"relationship"** a CEO is looking for. This helps me see if I want to be a long or a short-term investor in the business.

When I look for a CEO's attitude, I think about soul sister Aretha Franklin, who belted out a cry for R–E–S–P–E–C–T. Aretha knew the importance of this virtue. It's the basis of almost all successful partnerships.

Buffett knows this too. He respects investors. It shows when he uses simple language to explain complex concepts in his shareholder letters. He *talks with*, not *down to* investors. He's looking for investors who think of themselves as partners, not as holders of pieces of paper that can be dumped at the first sign of bad news. When he writes, "To the Shareholders of Berkshire Hathaway," he means fellow shareholders. In the 1996 Berkshire Hathaway Owner's Manual, Buffett described the long-term relationships he and Munger are seeking with their investors:

> *Charlie and I hope that you do not think of yourself as merely owning a piece of paper whose price wiggles around daily and that is a candidate for sale when some economic or political event makes you nervous. We hope you instead visualize yourself as a part owner of a business that you expect to stay with indefinitely,*

much as you might if you owned a farm or apartment house in partnership with members of your family. For our part, we do not view Berkshire shareholders as faceless members of an ever-shifting crowd, but rather as co-venturers who have entrusted their funds to us for what may well turn out to be the remainder of their lives.[1]

Dear Bertie and Doris

Practically all CEO letters are addressed to shareholders, but few CEOs will tell you precisely who they mean. Buffett told me that he imagines his sisters, Bertie and Doris, when he writes his shareholder letter. Like their famous brother, most of their net worth is invested in Berkshire Hathaway. They are intelligent and well-versed in business basics, but are not financial pros. Buffett imagines they have been out of the country and away from the media for a year. Consequently, they expect Buffett's letter to explain how the year's events affected the business and the value of their holdings.[2]

A good letter will refer to corporate goals from previous years and tell investors whether or not they've been met. For example in his 2000 letter, Buffett referred all the way back to 1983:

Many people assume that marketable securities are Berkshire's first choice when allocating capital, but that's not true: Ever since we first published our economic principles in 1983, we have consistently stated that we would rather purchase businesses than stocks. (See number 4 on page 60.) One reason for that preference is personal, in that I love working with our managers. They are high-grade, talented and loyal. And, frankly, I find their business behavior to be more rational and owner-oriented than that prevailing at many public companies.

My research shows that Buffett goes even further than other CEOs. In his 2000 letter, he identified with investors:

At Berkshire, full reporting means giving you the information that we would wish you to give to us if our positions were reversed. What Charlie and I would want under that circumstance would be all the important facts about current operations as well as the CEO's frank view of the long-term economic characteristics of the business. We would expect both a lot of financial details and a discussion of any significant data we would need to interpret what was presented...

Charlie and I tend to be leery of companies run by CEOs who woo investors with fancy predictions. A few of these managers will prove prophetic but others will turn out to be congenital optimists, or even charlatans. Unfortunately, it's not easy for investors to know in advance which species they are dealing with.

In my 2000 shareholder letter survey, only 29 percent of the CEOs identified with investors. Enron never did. My review of Enron's shareholder letters from 1996-2000 failed to spot any language indicating that the company identified with its customers *or* employees.

Enron's Shareholders Can't Keep Up

Rather than anticipating concerns, Kenneth Lay and Jeff Skilling, the former Chairman and CEO of Enron, started off their 1999 shareholder letter by suggesting that investors and market watchers were too slow to keep up with the company:

Enron is moving so fast that sometimes others have trouble defining us. But we know who we are. We are clearly a knowledge-based company, and the skills and resources we used to transform the energy business are proving to be equally valuable in other businesses. Yes, we will remain the world's leading energy company, but we also will use our skills and talents to gain leadership in fields where the right opportunities beckon.

This upfront arrogance is not characteristic of any other CEO letters. From 1996-2000, Enron made generic promises to provide superior shareholder value, increase shareholder wealth, and deliver strong results. All are admirable goals, but with nothing to back them up, they sound like hollow political slogans. In 1997, they promised to assist investors' understanding and analysis of their operations by continuing to "more clearly present the outstanding fundamentals of our operations." But there was no further mention of this laudable effort in the years that followed.

Investor Amnesia

In fact, there was little continuity in the Enron letters from one year to the next. Lay and Skilling may have assumed that their investors had amnesia or that they never held the stock longer than a year. Or perhaps, each year different individuals or teams were drafted to write the letters. Whatever the cause, this astonishing lack of consistency made it virtually impossible to compare statements about Enron's financial results from one year to the next. (See Chapter Six for a detailed discussion.)

Enron's 1996 shareholder letter described the company with minimum humility and maximum hubris:

> *We believe we are reinventing the energy business. We're not the biggest – yet. We're not the most profitable – yet. But we're changing energy possibilities – by expanding them.*

References to profits were becoming scarce by 1998. Increasingly, the CEO letters focused on top-line results, while paying scant attention to the bottom line. By 2000, the appearance of humility and the importance of profitability had all but disappeared. Skilling's 2000 letter was littered with jargon and hyperbole:

> *Enron hardly resembles the company we were in the early days. During our 15-year history, we have stretched ourselves beyond our own expectations. We have metamorphosed from an asset-based pipeline and power generating company to a marketing and logistics company whose biggest assets are its well-established business approach and its innovative people.*

A Clock with No Hands

To be fair to Enron and its investors, few people spent much time reading shareholder letters in the New Economy. During the fifteen-year bull market, money flowed too fast for people to pay attention to words.

It was the best of times and the best of times. A networked planet was expected to usher in a new age of global peace and understanding. Highly respected companies like Cisco Systems predicted that Internet technology was going to help solve world poverty. A web surfer in every hut was the technologist's impassioned version of the old political promise of a chicken in every pot. Overnight, people with both good and ill-conceived ideas gained reputable financial backing and became paper billionaires. Dot.com mania proved that investing was no more difficult than cooking instant soup.

At the height of this frenzy, respected financial analysts priced Internet companies as a multiple of their marketing costs. This New Economy math assumed that marketing expenses would automatically result in sales. Profits and principles were largely forgotten.

Buffett commented on this party atmosphere in his 2000 shareholder letter:

> *The line separating investment and speculation, which is never bright and clear, becomes blurred still further when most market participants have recently enjoyed triumphs. Nothing sedates rationality like large doses of effortless money. After a heady experience of that kind, normally sensible people drift into behavior akin to that of Cinderella at the ball. They know that overstaying the festivities – that is, continuing to speculate in companies that have gigantic valuations relative to the cash they are likely to generate in the future – will eventually bring on pumpkins and mice. But they nevertheless hate to miss a single minute of what is one helluva party. Therefore, the giddy participants all plan to leave just seconds before midnight. There's a problem, though: They are dancing in a room in which the clocks have no hands.*

When Companies Court the Market, Not Investors

In the world of New Economy investing, Enron was a star. Claiming that its biggest assets were its innovative approach and people, it sounded like a technology company, but also boasted earnings. Unlike companies whose sole asset was cash raised in IPOs, Enron offered investors a balance sheet that measured assets and liabilities in the billions. Compared to the dot.com competition, investors had to have more confidence owning Enron.

By including all of its energy trading activity as revenues, the company became the seventh largest in the S&P 500. But trading revenues are not like revenues that come from selling toothpaste or airplanes. Trading revenues are marked or priced to their market prices. Because trades can extend from a period of months to years, they show up on a company's income statement based on values related to current market conditions. If market conditions change, then the value of these revenues must be restated in subsequent years.

But in 1999 and 2000, few investors paid attention to profits and cash. Now the seventh largest company on the New York Stock Exchange, Enron had to be owned by the market index funds. As a result, demand for Enron's stock soared. In what Buffett calls "the sometimes foolish market," momentum begets momentum. How could you not buy Enron when everyone else around you was snapping it up? Enron defied the laws of economic gravity.

Gravity and Integrity

From the beginning of 1999 to the end of 2000, Enron's stock climbed 177 percent, from $30 to $83. Prominent sell-side equity analysts cranked out reports that rated Enron a "Strong Buy." But in early 2000, analysts privately began to admit that they couldn't figure out how Enron made money. Analysts and professional investors sedated themselves with the "hard" evidence of the company's record of consistent and explosive earnings per-share growth. They assumed that management was reporting numbers that could be trusted.

They were wrong. Not only Enron, but also other large and respected companies began to disclose aggressive accounting practices that stretched reports of their profits and cash flow beyond the limits of propriety and, possibly, the law.

Managing Earnings, Not Companies

Here's what Buffett wrote in 1998 about the growing gamesmanship in reporting corporate earnings:

It was once relatively easy to tell the good guys in accounting from the bad: The late 1960's, for example, brought on an orgy of what one charlatan dubbed "bold, imaginative accounting" (the practice of which, incidentally, made him loved for a time by Wall Street because he never missed expectations). But most investors of that period knew who was playing games. And, to their credit,

*virtually all of America's most-admired companies then shunned
deception.*

*In recent years, probity has eroded. Many major corporations still
play things straight, but a significant and growing number of
otherwise high-grade managers – CEOs you would be happy to
have as spouses for your children or as trustees under your will –
have come to the view that it's okay to manipulate earnings to
satisfy what they believe are Wall Street's desires. Indeed, many
CEOs think this kind of manipulation is not only okay, but
actually their duty.*

He wrote this passage three years before investors began seeing
the ugly consequences of these games.

Tortoise Investing

Admittedly, Warren Buffett's style of investing lacks
excitement. In this same 1998 shareholder letter, Buffett wrote that
he and Munger were content to stay at home doing the "easy jobs
at Berkshire":

*We do very little except allocate capital. And even then, we are not
all that energetic. We have one excuse, though: In allocating
capital, activity does not correlate with achievement. Indeed, in
the fields of investments and acquisitions, frenetic behavior is often
counterproductive. Therefore, Charlie and I mainly just wait for
the phone to ring.*

People who try to keep up in a bull market often confuse
investing with the purchase of a lottery ticket. With the NASDAQ
soaring, many shareholder letters should have been addressed to
Fellow Speculator, not *Fellow Investor.* Buffett described the
difference between speculation and investing in his 2000 letter:

*…there are many times when the most brilliant of investors can't
muster a conviction about* [valuing investments] *… not even
when a very broad range of estimates is employed. This kind of
uncertainty frequently occurs when new businesses and rapidly
changing industries are under examination. In cases of this sort,
any capital commitment must be labeled speculative.*

Now, speculation – in which the focus is not on what an asset will produce but rather on what the next fellow will pay for it – is neither illegal, immoral nor un-American. But it is not a game in which Charlie and I wish to play. We bring nothing to the party, so why should we expect to take anything home?

Paying the Price for Principles

In hindsight, Buffett was right. In the first year of the new millennium, most investors preferred riding on the easy money train. Refusing to invest in technology, Berkshire's stock tumbled from $80,000 in March 1999 down to $41,300 in March 2000. Buffett lost his ranking as the second richest man in the world.

While other CEOs might have limited their exposure to shareholders when their stock was tumbling, Buffett and Munger remained as visible as ever. At their 2000 Annual Shareholders Meeting, the two executives fielded investor questions in a six-hour open forum. Buffett had already anticipated some of the tough questions in his 11,635-word shareholder letter.

Maybe this explains why shareholder questions, under the circumstances, were relatively polite. One exception was a shareholder who suggested that Buffett and Munger receive "lashes with a wet noodle" for setting investor expectations so low. He queried: "Isn't there enough left in your brainpower to look into technology? I made over 100% in technology mutual funds…"

Buffett replied sharply, "Lots of people say they know how to invest in technology. Why would you have us invest in technology for you? Did you bring business cards?" He suggested that anyone interested in investing in technology should see this shareholder. [3]

Always the patient investor, Buffett weathered the storm. When I asked him if it was harder to write his letter when Berkshire's stock was heading south instead of north, he confessed, "I like the challenge of writing about a bad year." His 1999 letter offered no excuses for Berkshire's sub-par performance. At the start of that year's letter, he gave himself a "D" for capital allocation, his most important job as CEO.

On March 10, 2000, the day before his 1999 shareholder letter hit the streets, the NASDAQ index, which includes many New Economy stocks, reached its all-time high of 5,048 points.

Meanwhile, Berkshire Hathaway's stock was trading at a low of $41,300. But by the close of business on the first trading day in 2002, the NASDAQ was at 1,979 and Berkshire's stock traded at $74,300.

Just as Aesop observed thousands of years ago, never underestimate the tortoise. Investors who stuck with Buffett and Munger were vindicated and rewarded. Those who bought at the low point almost doubled their investment. They learned that R-E-S-P-E-C-T can also be spelled R-I-C-H.

Chapter Four

Auld Lang Syne:
Corporate Goals and Resolutions

GOAL. *Etymology: Middle English gol [boundary], Old English gal [barrier].*
1. the goal toward which effort is directed; an objective
2. the finish line or a race; a structure or zone into or over which players try to advance a ball or puck; the score awarded for such an act

(American Heritage College Dictionary, Third Edition)

"**Corporate goals**" are like New Year's resolutions. Everyone knows they're important. They can boost our performance. We like thinking of all the positive change that will result if we work hard to make them happen – less flab, better health, and more money. But we hate the work, we hate feeling the pressure of having to meet them and worst, we hate the idea of failing.

Maybe that's why so few CEOs disclose their company goals in investor communications. In my 2000 survey of shareholder letters, only 45 percent of the companies reported on their financial goals and only 38 percent reported any operating goals.

A CEO who wants to show that he or she is trying to be accountable to investors and other stakeholders is going to tell you about their corporate goals. It's easy to find them when the word "goal" is used, but I also look for words like "objective," "aim," or "target." These all tell me that a CEO has some defined and desired endgame.

Financial Goals

Financial goals reveal the financial targets that CEOs want their companies to achieve. There are many types. Look for financial goals related to earnings growth, total return, debt capitalization (how much debt a company carries relative to its equity), dividend payout or the returns that management wants to earn on the equity of the company and on its total invested capital. A good example is from Dow Chemical's 2000 annual letter (emphasis added):

> ...*we remain committed to our financial objectives. <u>We continue to be on track to meet our goals of earning 3 percent above our cost of capital and a 20 percent return on equity across the cycle.</u> And we have again surpassed <u>our toughest goal – that of earning the cost of capital at the bottom of the industry cycle</u>, as product prices have been unable to keep pace with the significant increase in feedstock costs. This level of performance truly differentiates us in our industry and is just one of the many factors that led the* Financial Times *and* Forbes *to recognize Dow as the world's most respected energy/chemicals company and the best chemical company in America, respectively.*

Operating Goals

Operating goals reveal the CEOs' aspirations to improve the way work gets done. They include productivity, customer service and efficiency goals. In its 2000 letter, Wells Fargo offered unusually detailed customer-related operating goals. These goals tell you how employees are keeping busy. They are written in a way that motivates employees, as well as informs the reader (emphasis added):

> ...*to grow revenue in double digits every year we must sell at least one more product to every customer every year. When Norwest and Wells Fargo merged in November 1998 our combined cross-sell was about 3.3 products per retail banking household. At year-end 2000, it was about 3.7. <u>To get to our goal of eight we need to double that. We're headed in the right direction but not fast enough.</u>*

> <u>*Our goal is to reduce – by at least half – the annual rate at which we're losing customers.*</u> *We lose one of every five consumers every year due primarily to failures in our processes or in our attitude. One of every five – gone! That may not be unusual for a financial services company but that doesn't make it acceptable. Cutting our annual customer loss by half would, alone, increase our revenue ten percent.*

Buffett stated three financial goals and three operating goals in his 2000 letter. Enron did not reveal any goals. In fact, over the past five years Enron's shareholder letters reported on only four goals in total. Not an impressive show of accountability.

But while the quantity of goal statements may be noteworthy, the quality is even more so. Over the years, I've observed three kinds of corporate goals. I call these "Motherhood," "Jaws" and "Masterpiece" goals. Like an Olympic judge, I rate goals by degrees of difficulty.

Motherhood Goals

Motherhood goals are generic in that they reveal little, but sound good. They exude the comfort of Motherhood and the aroma of apple pie. Enron's sole operating goal in 1999 is a good example of a Motherhood goal:

Our goal is to be the premier provider of high-bandwidth services and applications worldwide.

This sounds brave and bold, but it lacks any kind of performance standard. How can you tell if they have become the premier provider of high bandwidth services? They don't even tell you what high bandwidth looks like. I don't give a company much credit for telling me these kinds of goals.

Jaws Goals

Jaws goals, in contrast, have teeth. These have a higher degree of difficulty because they offer a performance standard. Enron's 1997 letter expressed their goals in stronger language. It defined the kinds of results they were seeking to achieve (emphasis added):

Although our business portfolio will continue to provide periodic opportunities to capture non-recurring values, we are committed to generating strong, visible and predictable recurring earnings growth year after year.

We also are committed to delivering earnings growth from our core businesses in 1998 and target an approximate 10 percent increase over 1997 earnings. This growth will exclude one-time earnings items.

Masterpiece Goals

Masterpiece goals have the highest degree of difficulty. These goals not only have teeth, they also tell you something original and enduring about the company. Buffett is the master of Masterpiece goals. Here's what he wrote in 2000 (emphasis added):

> Charlie and I continue to _aim at increasing Berkshire's per-share value_ at a rate that, over time, will modestly exceed the gain from owning the S&P 500. As the table on the facing page shows, a small annual advantage in our favor can, if sustained, produce an anything-but-small long-term advantage. _To reach our goal_ we will need to add a few good businesses to Berkshire's stable each year, have the businesses we own generally gain in value, and avoid any material increase in our outstanding shares. We are confident about meeting the last two objectives; the first will require some luck.

In these four sentences Buffett:

→ provides a specific performance measure – per-share value – which he subsequently defines as the per-share book value and per-share intrinsic value;

→ provides a measure against which to measure this performance: exceed the gain from owning the S&P 500;

→ tells the readers three things Berkshire must do to meet this goal;

→ candidly assesses their chances of attaining the goal;

→ shows that he and Munger are holding themselves personally accountable for the results.

Unlike Motherhood goals, Jaws and Masterpiece goals are investor-friendly. They provide standards that allow us to see if companies are meeting their goals.

Chapter Five

Meat and Potatoes:

Linking Goals With Results

ACCOUNT/ACCOUNTABILITY. *from Middle English, Old French acont, aconter [to reckon]; from Latin ad + cunter [to count]*
1. *a narrative or record of events; a reason given for a particular action*
2. *a formal banking, brokerage, or business relationship established to provide for financial transactions; a precise list or enumeration of financial transactions; money deposited for checking, savings, or brokerage use; a customer having a business or credit relationship with a firm*
3. *to provide an explanation or justification for*
4. *to hold answerable for*

(American Heritage College Dictionary, Third Edition)

Companies in deep trouble, Enron-style deep trouble, know the importance of credit. Enron lacked financial credit to borrow money when it urgently needed capital. Dynegy, the company that offered to buy Enron pulled out of the deal after exercising due diligence. Bankruptcy was inevitable.

The word credit comes from the Latin word *credere* which means "to believe." Not many people realize that our tough, hard-asset business world is ultimately based on something as fragile and intangible as belief. Companies that operate with integrity build financial and psychological credit reserves to draw upon when trouble hits.

CEOs who hold themselves accountable for their company's promises and actions build trust. I spot integrity in a shareholder letter when a CEO tells me how his or her company is **"linking their goals with their results."** This accountability topic is the meat and potatoes of a shareholder letter.

Checking Up on Past Promises

Remember CEO Kenneth Lay's promise in Enron's 1997 shareholder letter to grow earnings at ten percent per year? He never bothered to mention this goal and Enron met it in his 1998 letter. It makes you wonder. Same CEO and company. Forgotten promise. Do other CEOs review past promises? Not usually.

I used to be cynical and think that this head-in-the-sand ostrich maneuver was deliberate. But after working in this area for years, I've found that this failure to revisit the past is often an oversight. Among the companies I worked with, only one routinely started its new shareholder letter by reviewing the previous year's letter. Almost everyone else acted as if the new year's letter was a blank slate and a fresh start.

Few CEOs Are Serving Meat and Potatoes

Few companies expect readers to go back to check past promises. Instead, they describe a goal in their letter (regardless of whether it was mentioned in a previous letter) and tell you how or if they met that goal.

In my 2000 survey of shareholder letters, I found that only 38 percent of the CEOs linked their goals with results. The Burlington Northern Santa Fe Corporation (BNSF) earned the highest marks for providing detailed information about their goals and the performance measurements to show how the company was meeting them. They earned points because they discussed:

Meeting Safety Goals

At BNSF, we want to achieve our potential, but we want to do it safely. That's the mark of true leadership and our commitment to our employees, customers and the public. We believe safety and efficiency go hand-in-hand. Our goal is to have an injury-free, accident free workplace.

Our progress toward this goal since 1995 has been outstanding. Employee injury frequency and severity (lost work days) ratios, as measured per 200,000 hours worked, have dropped 12 percent and 52 percent, respectively, in this five-year period. This reduction in severity reflects approximately 22,000 fewer lost workdays in 2000 compared with 1995, or the equivalent of 110 full-time employees.

BNSF also wrote extensively about its goals to improve customer service, reliability, and efficiency:

Meeting Customer Service Goals

Providing consistent on time service to our customers is the key to revenue growth and realizing our potential. We have changed our business processes to make it easier for customers to do business with BNSF. We invested more than $500 million since 1995 to develop, expand and enhance our real time integrated information system as well as to constantly expand our suite of web based applications.

Goal to Increase Reliability and Predictability

But BNSF's most significant efficiency initiatives took place in our mechanical and engineering departments in 2000. Together, the departments saved approximately $130 million by identifying and removing "waste" from numerous processes associated with maintaining our locomotives, freight cars, track, signals and bridges. Our goal is to increase the reliability and predictability of our fleets and all of our physical assets in order to execute flawlessly the transportation service plan (TSP) for every car on our system based on our customers' needs.

Efficiency Goals

Since 1995, BNSF has increased the annual number of gross ton miles (GTMs) it handles at a faster rate than other Class I railroads. Gross ton miles, a standard industry measure, reflect the total tons of freight hauled and the distance the freight was moved. Over the past five years, GTMs increased 17 percent to 875 billion. For the same period, adjusted operating expense per 1,000 GTMs declined 14 percent to $7.20 adjusted for inflation.

Enron made no such effort to link the company's goals with results in its 2000 shareholder letter. Berkshire scored high in this category. For each of the past five years, Buffett has reported on how well or how poorly Berkshire has fared in meeting its goals of increasing net worth and intrinsic value.

What about Enron? You have to go back to its 1996 shareholder letter to find such forthright disclosure:

Our infrastructure business currently has three large power projects valued at $3 billion in construction. Three more power projects, targeted to start in 1997, are valued at over $1 billion. They're part of a backlog of more than $20 billion in high quality projects.

Our wholesale and retail electricity marketing activities are off to a tremendous start. So are our LNG infrastructure projects, which are working to deliver clean natural gas to India, the Middle East and Puerto Rico.

Each of these new businesses, as well as our renewable energy business, is targeting a net present value of at least $1 billion or more by early in the next decade. And these businesses – which we were not in five years ago – are on track to generate 40 percent of our net income five years from now.

There are teeth in these goals. Enron expected these new businesses to throw off impressive cash flow ($1.0 billion in net present values for each) and to contribute substantially to overall net income. The problem is you had to stick around for five years to see if they succeeded in meeting these goals. After 1996, neither of these goals was mentioned again. Investors were never told if Enron was on track to meet them.

Berkshire Hathaway: Consistency Breeds Confidence

Here is what Buffett wrote in his 1996 letter to describe meeting the Berkshire goal of increasing its per-share book value:

Our gain in net worth during 1996 was $6.2 billion, or 36.1%. Per-share book value, however, grew by less, 31.8%, because the number of Berkshire shares increased: We issued stock in acquiring FlightSafety International and also sold new Class B shares. Over the last 32 years (that is, since present management took over) per-share book value has grown from $19 to $19,011, or at a rate of 23.8% compounded annually.

Here is what Buffett wrote in 2000:

Our gain in net worth during 2000 was $3.96 billion, which increased the per-share book value of both our Class A and Class B stock by 6.5%. Over the last 36 years (that is, since present *management took over) per-share book value has grown from $19 to $40,442, a gain of 23.6% compounded annually.*

Sound familiar? In each of the past five years, Buffett reported on Berkshire's progress in meeting the goal of growth in per-share value. In recent years, he has emphasized the importance of growth that exceeds the gain from owning the S&P 500.

In 1996, Buffett did something that no other CEO in our survey has ever done. He tried to dampen investor expectations about Berkshire's future growth:

Our expectations, however, are tempered by two realities. First, our past rates of growth cannot be matched nor even approached: Berkshire's equity capital is now large – in fact, fewer than ten businesses in America have capital larger – and an abundance of funds tends to dampen returns. Second, whatever our rate of progress, it will not be smooth: Year-to-year moves in the first column of the table (the amount of investments per share) above will be influenced in a major way by fluctuations in securities markets; the figures in the second column (the per share earnings of operating companies) will be affected by wide swings in the profitability of our catastrophe-reinsurance business.

These cautions were repeated each subsequent year. His prediction that earnings would be affected by the profitability of the catastrophic insurance business finally came true in 2001 when Berkshire announced its first loss in net worth in the history of the company. Were investors alarmed by this news? Although Berkshire's stock dropped approximately 10 percent in price after the World Trade Center attacks, it rebounded to its pre-September 11th value only two weeks later. Investors had been forewarned.

The Five-Year Test

Professional investors tell me that they keep the last five years of a company's annual reports on file. Buffett and other professional investors look for consistency when they read shareholder letters from year to year. CEOs who engage in an ongoing dialogue in their letters get credibility points from them and my company. But since so few letters reference the past, investors are often disappointed.

In his 1996 letter, Buffett wrote about another long-standing Berkshire Hathaway goal – fair treatment for all investors:

> *Though our primary goal is to maximize the amount that our shareholders, in total, reap from their ownership of Berkshire, we wish also to minimize the benefits going to some shareholders at the expense of others. These are goals we would have were we managing a family partnership, and we believe they make equal sense for the manager of a public company. In a partnership, fairness requires that partnership interests be valued equitably when partners enter or exit; in a public company, fairness prevails when market price and intrinsic value are in sync. Obviously, they won't always meet that ideal, but a manager – by his policies and communications – can do much to foster equity.*

That year, Berkshire issued a new Class B stock that allowed people to own a piece of the company at a much-reduced price. It did so to thwart attempts by others to market a trust security that looked like Berkshire stock, but which would have unfairly inflated the price of the Class A stock. The investors who figured out they could reap a windfall by selling their stock would have gained, but the investors who did not sell, would have been disadvantaged. Buffett feared over time that increased investor traffic would erode confidence in the company.

Five years later, Buffett still writes about treating all shareholders fairly. Here's an excerpt from his 2000 shareholder letter about the importance of "fair reporting" to investors:

> *For us, fair reporting means getting information to our 300,000 "partners" simultaneously, or as close to that mark as possible. We therefore put our annual and quarterly financials on the Internet between the close of the market on a Friday and the following morning. By our doing that, shareholders and other interested investors have timely access to these important releases and also have a reasonable amount of time to digest the information they include before the markets open on Monday. This year our quarterly information will be available on the Saturdays of May 12, August 11, and November 10. The 2001 annual report will be posted on March 9.*

Holding CEOs Accountable

In 1999, 29 percent of the companies in my shareholder letter survey mentioned goals. In 2000, less than half of these same companies reported to investors about whether they had realized these goals or made progress in meeting them.

What were the non-reporting CEOs thinking? Obviously they acted as if no one would notice their failure to review earlier promises.

Do investors mind? Institutional investors holding large positions in companies have easy access to top management. If they have a question about whether or not a company is meeting its goals, they pick up the phone and ask it. If the answer doesn't suit them, they can vote with their feet and sell their stock. That's easier than raising a ruckus. Investment fund managers are paid handsomely to boost investment returns, not to change the behavior of management.

What about individual investors? Few take action. We're all too busy or too intimidated by management to believe that we could make a difference.

Years ago, I coached the head of investor relations for a large company. This person had the thankless job of drafting the CEO letter. When I asked him to consider addressing the company's progress at meeting its goals, he looked at me quizzically and said, "Why bother? No one reads these letters any way."

They do now.

Chapter Six

Will the Real Earnings Please Stand Up?
Financial Results

EARN/EARNINGS. *Etymology: Middle English ernen, from Old English earnian; akin to Old High German arnOn to reap. Date: before 12th century [1752, earnings]*
1. *to receive as return for effort and especially for work done or services rendered: to bring in by way of return*
2. *something (as wages) earned*
3. *the balance of revenue after deduction of costs and expenses*
   (Merriam-Webster Online Collegiate Dictionary)

When companies report on linking goals with results, there is no result more important than the **"year-end earnings."** Earnings are the oxygen of business. Cut off the supply and the business dies. To appreciate how earnings results are reported in a CEO letter, you'll need to understand the company's income statement. This can be found in the financial statements in the annual report.

Sizing Up the Income Statement
Think of the income statement as a financial report card that answers a simple question: Did a company make money or lose money? The answer to this question is the company's "bottom line."

The income statement looks like a shopping list. The first line, called a "line item," shows *revenues*. This tells us the total dollar value of all company sales. Revenues include both the sales of tangible products, like consumer goods, and the sales of intangibles, such as fees for services. When people talk about top-line growth, they're describing a company's growth in revenues from year to year.

Move down the list to find the company's expenses. Generally, there are two forms of expenses: those related to the direct cost of making a product and indirect expenses related to the cost of running the business. These include the CEO's salary, accountant fees, and marketing and advertising expenses.

When you add up all the money that came in during the year and subtract the money that went out to run the business, you're left with the company's "net earnings" or "net income." Net earnings measure the company's bottom line. This is the CEO's *most* important grade on the financial report card. Positive earnings are reported in black ink; negative earnings in red ink. Black ink means the CEO received a passing grade, red ink means failure.

Price Earnings Envy

Company earnings not only measure company performance, they also determine the price of the company's stock. Companies that report better earnings are supposed to trade at a higher *price earnings ratio (P/E)* than other companies. Earnings are the E in the P/E ratio. Many terms are used to describe P/E ratios, such as "price earnings multiple" or simply, "multiple." They all mean the same thing.

To calculate the P/E ratio, first figure out a company's per share earnings. For example, assume that a company has $200 million in earnings and also has 100 million shares of stock outstanding. When you divide these earnings by the number of shares you will get $2.00 in per share earnings (EPS). Now assume that the company's stock is trading at $30. Take this number and divide by the EPS to get P/E ratio of 15. This tells you that investors are willing to pay 15 times earnings to own the company's stock.

While some analysts use current earnings to measure the P/E ratio, most prefer to peg the price earnings multiple to an estimate of future earnings. Equity analysts run quantitative models to estimate future earnings. They evaluate soft factors such as management credibility, a company's competitive advantage, and market demand for their product. A high P/E indicates investor confidence in the company's ability to deliver on their earnings promises.

In 2000 for example, Enron was trading at an average P/E multiple of about 56. In other words, investors were willing to pay

56 times the amount of Enron's year-end earnings to own the stock.

Many companies were green with Enron Envy. They wanted to trade at its multiple because it gave them an advantage in acquiring other companies. For example, if your stock trades at a 15 multiple and you use that stock to acquire the stock of another company that trades at a 10 multiple, you are essentially buying that company for a 50 percent discount.

Many people invested in Enron because of its high P/E multiple. Believing in the wisdom of the market, they never did their homework or due diligence on the company. Investors who paid attention to such things would have noticed that when Enron traded at around 60 times earnings, the index of companies in the S&P 500 was trading at only between 23 to 25 times this index's composite earnings.

These investors reacted to Enron's sky-high P/E with alarm rather than celebration. Focusing on the E and not the P, these financial sleuths went straight to the footnotes in Enron's financial statements. They pieced together a more accurate picture of the company's earnings and prospects. Many of these investors were spared the financial carnage to come.

But what can investors do when they don't know how to decipher financial footnotes? I believe many could still have been alerted to potential problems by carefully reading the earnings language in Enron's shareholder letters from 1996 to 2000.

An Open, Not a Shut Case

When companies responsibly report their earnings in their shareholder letters, investors gain greater confidence in the governance of the corporation. In fact, it is so important you would expect to find this information in every CEO letter. Not so. Forty-two percent of the CEO letters in our 2000 survey didn't even mention company earnings.

In other words, these CEOs neglected to tell you their "bottom line" grade for the year. Investors can only wonder if this omission was deliberate or an oversight. When such vital information is missing, investors can reasonably ask what the CEO may be trying to hide.

Even when CEOs do report company earnings, it's often hard to figure out what they mean. Earnings are described in many different ways. You may find one or more of the following:

Operating earnings
Net earnings or net income
Earnings per share
Recurring earnings
Non-recurring earnings
Diluted earnings per share

After trying to wade through this linguistic quagmire, a frustrated investor may understandably throw up his or her hands and shout, "Will the real earnings please stand up?"

GAAP vs. Pro forma Earnings

You can blame part of this problem on accounting. While accounting used to be a cure for insomnia, it's now a cause for sleeplessness. To find out if you're doing business with someone whose numbers you can understand and also trust, it may be useful to think about the Grand Canyon. The Canyon itself is made up of different geological strata. Think of these strata as levels of earnings. Ultimately, an investor wants to know how many levels he has to pass through to get to the bottom of the canyon. To gain confidence in your investment, you want a CEO who gives you earnings information that can guide you down as close as possible to the banks of the mighty Colorado River.

Many companies choose to report their earnings in shareholder letters several layers up from the riverbank. Typically they select a layer that lets them show their company's earnings in the best possible light. This is not illegal. It falls within the rules of the Generally Accepted Accounting Principles (GAAP) that have been established by the accounting profession to standardize corporate reporting. But when companies offer these customized Pro forma earnings that stray from GAAP, a careful investor will want to examine the underlying assumptions the company is using to calculate them. It's prudent to question management about the size of the gap between their GAAP and Pro forma earnings.

Accounting Games: Recurring and Non-Recurring Earnings

Smart investors know that figuring out the difference between recurring and non-recurring earnings can help them analyze this gap. Companies engage in creative accounting because they get to choose how to record certain gains and losses. Both result from business operations, but the accounting for them differs. A loss associated with "normal" windfalls or mistakes is spread out over time. Non-routine or extraordinary gains and losses (i.e., highly unlikely to recur) are called *non-recurring charges* or *gains*. This type of loss is written off all at once. The former are *recurring charges*.

Companies "manage" earnings by choosing how to classify these losses and gains. For example, when the costs of mistakes are included in a single accounting period, companies get to show a lousy one-time earnings result. The alternative approach – to expense these costs over time – reduces future earnings. Managements often choose one-time write-offs, preferring to get the bad news behind them.

But critics argue that this practice distorts the true picture of the business value. Cisco's write-off of $2.5 billion in inventory in 2001 is one controversial example of taking such a write-off. Some business experts believe that misjudging inventory is a routine cost of business. Liquidating this inventory by taking annual charges against income would more accurately reflect the ongoing value of Cisco's business. Cisco decided otherwise.

Buffett described the problem of accounting for *restructuring charges* in his 1998 letter:

> *The distortion du jour is the "restructuring charge," an accounting entry that can, of course, be legitimate but that too often is a device for manipulating earnings. In this bit of legerdemain, a large chunk of costs that should properly be attributed to a number of years is dumped into a single quarter, typically one already fated to disappoint investors. In some cases, the purpose of the charge is to clean up earnings misrepresentations of the past, and in others it is to prepare the ground for future misrepresentations. In either case, the size and timing of these charges is dictated by the cynical proposition that Wall Street will not mind if earnings fall short by $5 per share in a given quarter, just as long as this deficiency*

ensures that quarterly earnings in the future will consistently exceed expectations by five cents per share.

Putting this activity into a meaningful context, Buffett cited a study that compared the amount of special charges either taken or announced in 1998 to the total net earnings reported by all the *Fortune 500* companies in 1997. Incredibly, these special charges, added up to $72.1 billion. This number equaled almost one-fifth of all reported 1997 earnings. Four years later, the costly consequences of robbing Peter to pay Paul are rattling investors' faith in the entire accounting profession.

I recommend that investors look for two indicators in shareholder letters to judge management's accounting integrity:

→ Clarity in reporting the nature of non-routine write-offs that affect company earnings

→ Consistency in the presentation of earnings over time.

Clarity and Consistency: Enron's Earnings

Enron's earnings statements from its 1996-2000 shareholder letters offer an excellent case study in creative earnings reporting. Over this five-year period, they failed to report earnings clearly and consistently. I've added headlines to the following examples that illustrate how difficult it was for anyone to track Enron's earnings from year to year.

1996: Enron Omits Earnings Results, Reports Earnings Expectations

Enron's 1996 letter failed to mention any earnings results – not earnings per share, not operating earnings, and not net income. Instead, Enron described the growth expectations of the company's *earnings per share,* pegging this at annual double-digit rates for the next five years (emphasis added):

> *We expect to achieve compound annual growth in earnings per share of at least 15 percent from 1996 through the year 2000. We expect minimum double digit earnings per share growth every year during that time.*

The company did offer one other measure of financial performance: improving its credit quality. This ratio of debt to total capitalization is key to determining the company's ability to borrow money (emphasis added):

> *Our confidence is rooted too in our experience. It was barely twelve years ago that we took the building blocks of two sizable but distinctly different companies, and began to change the history of the industry. When, in 1985, we merged Houston Natural Gas and InterNorth into a company with $2 billion in market value, our debt to total capitalization was 73 percent. We moved to build off of our existing assets to grow new businesses. <u>The result: at year end 1996 we were a company with $11 billion in market value and a 38 percent debt to total capitalization.</u>*

But 1996 is the last time Enron mentions improving credit quality in a shareholder letter. By the end of 2001, a deeply troubled Enron knocked on the doors of the credit agencies to get the ratings it needed to issue more debt. But no one was willing to answer and let them in.

1997: Enron Reports Net Income of $0.32 Per Diluted Share

Only one year after Enron proclaimed its new earnings per-share growth goal of double-digit growth, the company missed its target (emphasis added):

> *<u>Our net income of $0.32 per diluted share included $1.82 per share of non-recurring charges primarily attributable to the renegotiation of a North Sea gas contract</u>. These financial results adversely affected our stock price performance, as 1997 total return to shareholders of (1.5) percent was our first annual negative return since 1991 – a year where the S&P 500 also showed a negative return.*

Now they didn't tell you they missed the target. That information was omitted. Instead, they used a new measure of performance: *net income per diluted share.* This measure requires you to adjust the denominator of the earnings per share calculation. To get diluted net income, you divide the net income by both the shares outstanding and shares related to the stock options that the company has authorized, but not issued.

This per share number is always going to be lower than the non-diluted earnings per share number. For example, go to the footnotes on page 83 in J.P. Morgan Chase & Co.'s 2001 Annual Report and you'll find that in 2001 the company reported net income per share of $0.83. But they also tell you the diluted net income figure of $0.80, which is calculated by adding 51.2 million option shares to the company's 1,972.4 million outstanding shares. In 2000, the difference between the diluted and non-diluted EPS was $.13 a share. Because this diluted earnings number is going to be lower, most companies fail to mention it in their shareholder letter.

I give CEOs extra credit when they do. Unless the company's fortunes decline precipitously, these optionable shares will eventually be cashed in. It's a real cost to shareholders and is highly useful information to get a true picture of corporate earnings. To Enron's credit, they report this in the 1997 shareholder letter.

But this positive development is offset by the company's failure to describe the details of the $1.82 per share "non-recurring" loss caused by the renegotiation of a North Sea contract. Without this information, it's not possible for us to judge if this is a routine or non-routine event. Everyone knows that losing $1.82 per share from one business contract reflects either a whopping failure of judgment or really bad luck. Without disclosing the nature of this problem, an investor can neither gain confidence that it has been fixed, nor that it will not be repeated.

1998: Enron Reports a 36 Percent Increase in Operating Income

In 1998's letter, Enron discarded this 1997 measure of diluted per share recurring earnings (emphasis added):

> In 1998, the business platform we have built to achieve that status delivered record earnings and excellent shareholder returns, outpacing our industry group and the broader stock market. _Earnings of $698 million from operations represent a 36 percent increase compared to 1997_, and our return to shareholders of almost 40 percent beat the 2.9 percent return of our peer group and the S&P 500 return of 28 percent.

Now readers were asked to focus on the 36 percent increase in earnings from Enron's operations. (Technically speaking, operating earnings are the income that is left over after deducting operating earnings are the income that is left over after deducting direct expenses, but before subtracting interest, taxes and also non-recurring charges.) But if you go to the income statement in the annual report, you won't find the $698 million number listed anywhere. The GAAP-based net income number is listed on the income statement as $703 million.

What's the reason for this difference? To figure this out you have to go to the notes that precede the income statement. This is called "Management's Discussion of Financial Condition and Results of Operations" (MD&A). In the first note you can spot the $703 million. It is listed as "after-tax results before items impacting comparability"– yet another new term for earnings. This mouthful means that the earnings figure in the shareholder letter doesn't match the number in Enron's GAAP income statement.

You can reconcile the difference between $698 million and $703 million. It is due to "non-recurring events" in 1998. In the MD&A footnote, you will see that these gains and losses netted out to a total increase of $5.0 million.

1999: Net Income Before Non-Recurring Items

In Enron's 1999 shareholder letter, the company used yet another new measure of earnings performance: *net income before non-recurring items* (emphasis added):

> *We reported another round of impressive financial and operating results. In 1999 revenue increased 28 percent to $40 billion, and* net income before non-recurring items increased 37 percent to reach $957 million.

Again, you won't find the number $957 million on their income statement. The net income number that conforms to GAAP accounting principles is listed as $893 million on the income statement. The gap between these numbers has grown. What's the reason? Flipping forward to the notes in the MD&A, we find the $957 million number.

In other words, Enron reported earnings in the shareholder letter that failed to take account of the "non-recurring" charges. In 1999, these charges resulted from gains on the sales of subsidiary stock, losses due to revised pricing of MBTE, a gasoline additive and losses due to an accounting restatement. These net out to a $64 million loss.

For the first time, the 1999 CEO letter mentions revenue increase as a measure of performance. Investors take note! When companies begin to give more page space to top-line growth than to bottom-line profits, it's prudent to wonder what management may *not* be telling you. Enron's earnings are no longer described as linked to activities such as "building off their assets," or from a "business platform" or even a North Sea contract. They seem to materialize out of thin air.

2000: Net Income Reached a Record $1.3 Billion

Enron's year 2000 shareholder letter started off with bold descriptions of significant top-line growth at a number of its business subsidiaries (emphasis added):

> *Enron's performance in 2000 was a success by any measure, as we continued to outdistance the competition and solidify our leadership in each of our major businesses. In our largest business, wholesale services, we experienced an enormous increase of 59 percent in physical energy deliveries. Our retail energy business achieved its highest level ever of total contract value. Our newest business, broadband services, significantly accelerated transaction activity, and our oldest business, the interstate pipelines, registered increased earnings. The company's net income reached a record $1.3 billion in 2000.*

Yet only one of Enron's business subsidiaries reported growth in earnings. The other three described growth in business activity without linking this to either earnings or sales. The company claimed that *net income reached a record $1.3 billion* in 2000, but that's not what you will find when you go to the audited financial statements. There the net income is reported as $979 million. As in 1999, no mention is made of any "non-recurring charges" in the shareholder letter or in the income statement. Return to the MD&A notes to look for that strange category called "after-tax results before items impacting comparability." There you'll find a $326 million charge listed "to reflect impairment of Azurix," an investment in a water company that, pardon the pun, was substantially underwater.

Later in this shareholder letter, Enron mentions recurring earnings as a concept, but it provides no specific numbers.

Enron is increasing earnings per share and continuing our strong returns to shareholders. Recurring earnings per share have increased steadily since 1997 and were up 25 percent in 2000.

But why does Enron pick the year 1997? Isn't this the year Enron had its problem with the North Sea contract? Compared to 1997 most earnings would look great! Pick a low base and you can always show a higher percentage improvement.

Earnings and Value

Five years of inconsistent and unclear earnings reports ought to give any prudent investor reasons to question management's claims. If you can't trust the earnings reports, you'll never know the true underlying value of the company.

When company earnings are presented in ways that diverge from accounting principles, it's less likely that the accounting numbers accurately reflect the cash in the business. Investors beware! Buffett constantly reminds Berkshire Hathaway investors that accounting earnings is the beginning, not the endpoint in trying to estimate a company's underlying value.

In the wake of the Enron collapse and the careful scrutiny of the accounting practices of many large and respected companies, investors are starting to notice something not surprising to Buffett. When companies depart from following principled accounting standards, the gap between the reported earnings and company cash flow may be widening.

Chapter Seven

Just Say the Magic Word:
Cash

CASH. *Etymology: modification of Middle French or Old Italian; Middle French casse [money box], from Old Italian cassa, from Latin capsa, [case].*
Date: 1596
1. *money in the form of bills or coins; currency*
2. *payment for goods or services in currency or by check; to exchange for or convert into ready money*
                  (American Heritage College Dictionary, Third Edition)

Groucho Marx and his zany brothers made films that kept people laughing during America's Great Depression in the 1930s. He later hosted a 1950s television game show called *You Bet Your Life.* At the start of each show, a magic word was revealed to his live studio audience, but not to the contestant. If the contestant said this word during the show, a plucked rubber duck dropped down in front of his or her startled face, Groucho flicked his cigar, and everyone applauded. The guest won $50 for saying the word.

In my analysis of shareholder letters, I reward CEOs who use a very specific four-letter magic word. My magic word never changes. It's **"cash."**

Consider the magic of compounding: If you had won $50 in 1950 and invested it at a compound rate of 22.6 percent (the average return earned by Berkshire's shareholders since Buffett took over the company in 1965) it would today be worth over $429,000, adjusted for inflation. This is the kind of magic that Buffett likes to practice. It's why he is laser-focused on cash.

Cash Conscious and Unconscious

Buffett used the word "cash" 12 times in his 2000 shareholder letter, more than any other CEO in our survey. Examine this powerful statement about cash flow:

...we completed two significant acquisitions that we negotiated in 1999 and initiated six more. All told, these purchases have cost us about $8 billion, with 97% of that amount paid in cash and 3% in stock. The eight businesses we've acquired have aggregate sales of about $13 billion and employ 58,000 people. Still, we incurred no debt in making these purchases, and our shares outstanding have increased only 1/3 of 1%. Better yet, we remain awash in liquid assets and are both eager and ready for even larger acquisitions.

It's simple: multiply .97 times $8 billion and you'll find that Berkshire spent $7.76 billion in cash to buy eight businesses that produced $13 billion in sales.

In contrast, Enron made one reference to cash in its 2000 shareholder letter. It was a "trust me" allusion revealing little: "The pipelines continued to provide strong earnings and cash flow in 2000." Over the past five years of Enron's shareholder letters, you'd find the word "cash" mentioned only six times. In other words, Buffett mentioned cash twice as many times in one year as Enron did in five.

But these statements refer only to the cash thrown off by Enron's natural gas transportation business – its bread-and-butter business. The cash flows produced by its new fast-growing Online and Broadband businesses were never mentioned.

Laser-Focused on Cash

Buffett prefers to invest in companies where managements are focused on cash: cash earnings, ongoing cash flow from the business operations, or cash from borrowing. Unfortunately, few shareholder letters offer convincing proof that CEOs are cash-focused.

Over half of the 100 CEOs in our 2000 survey even failed to mention the word "cash" in their shareholder letters. And only nine offered the kind of detailed reporting about cash that is provided by aerospace giant Lockheed Martin:

In 2000, we committed the Corporation to managing for cash and reducing debt. Free cash flow increased from approximately $875 million in 1999 to $1.8 billion in 2000, our best performance ever. This accomplishment was achieved mainly through the reduction of days working capital as we focused on the management of *receivables, customer advances, payables and inventory throughout all our business areas. By combining free cash flow with the $2 billion of cash proceeds from our divestitures, we reduced our debt by $2 billion and increased our cash invested by $1 billion. This brought our net-debt-to-capital ratio down from 64% to 54% and we are making rapid progress toward bringing this ratio within a preferred range of 40% to 50%.*

In this one paragraph they tell you about the:

→ one billion dollar increase in free cash flow;

→ improvements in the management of inventory, customer advances and accounts receivables to increase cash flow and;

→ cash that is used to reduce debt to improve the company's capitalization ratios.

Managing Cash Flow

Understanding how cash flow works is simple. You just need to know how cash enters and leaves a business. There are four ways that cash comes into a business:

→ showing a profit;

→ borrowing;

→ selling assets or parts of their business and;

→ issuing and selling stock.

The other part of the cash flow equation requires you to know how cash leaves a business. Cash flows out to pay:

→ the expenses to run the business;

→ dividends to the shareholders.

Whatever is left over (more is left if a company doesn't pay a dividend or pays only a small one) is reinvested in the business. This can be used to buy new equipment, new companies or parts of companies. (Berkshire does not pay a dividend because Buffett expects to deliver higher returns to investors than they could otherwise earn by investing the dividends themselves.)

Cash flow is defined in a number of different ways in CEO letters: operating cash flow, net cash flow and net pre-tax cash flow. Lockheed uses a rigorous term, "free cash flow."

To calculate this number you start with operating cash flow. This is the company's net income with the amortization and depreciation expenses added back since they are not real cash outlays like salaries and interest costs. Then you deduct capital expenditures.

Companies like Lockheed know that while depreciation may not be a real cash expense, it costs real money to replace large equipment. That's why they deduct the cash for capital expenditures. Then they deduct dividends, the cash paid out to shareholders. What's left is called *retained earnings*. This is the number that Warren Buffett focuses on: the dollars that will be used to grow future earnings.

Keeping Track of the Cash: A Balancing Act

You may begin to see the problem business people have in keeping track of the cash. Accounting for cash is like trying to pin a wave on the sand. Like a wave, cash constantly ebbs and flows in the business. So accountants choose a particular point in time and count how much cash is in the business at that moment. That number shows up on the balance sheet in the financial section of the company's annual report.

To master a balance sheet, you need to remember the difference between left and right. Assets that a business owns or controls are recorded on the left side of the balance sheet. The liabilities or everything a business must pay out, including the stockholder equity, get recorded on the right side.

Luca Pacioli, an Italian mathematician known as "the Father of Accounting," was the first to write about the concept of a balance sheet in 1494. His double-entry method of bookkeeping – balancing what a company owns or controls against the value of what it owes – is not a perfect system, but it's the best we've got. In fact, it hasn't changed much since the fifteenth century.[1]

To reflect a business transaction using this method, entries are made on each side of the balance sheet. For example, if you borrow $1 million for five years from a bank, you record an increase in your long-term debt (on the right side) and an increase in the value of your cash (on the left side under assets).

Too Much Debt Is a Drag on Cash Flow

When you know the amount of cash in a business, you know how liquid it is. A highly liquid business can pay off its debts without difficulty. To get a true picture of *business liquidity*, compare the amount of cash and cash-equivalents (left side of the balance sheet) with the amount of short-term debt and liabilities that a business owes (right side of the balance sheet). If the amount of short-term borrowing and liabilities is greater than or equal to the amount of cash and other short-term assets, you've found a business that may be headed for trouble.

In the previous example, Lockheed reminded investors that it is paying attention to this relationship by reporting its capital ratio. It's paying attention to its longer-term liquidity. This *capitalization ratio* is calculated by dividing what a company owes by the amount of equity in the business. If the debt-to-equity ratio is high, it means that it will be harder for the company to borrow more money. If the ratio is low, people are eager to lend it cash.

Cash-Pure and Cash-Poor: Accounting for Acquisitions

Buffett made eight references to cash when he talked about what he paid to buy the eight businesses Berkshire acquired in 2000. Buffett is almost obsessive about paying cash to buy companies rather than issuing stock. This shows he is living up to two strongly held principles: 1) don't dilute the interests of current shareholders by issuing more stock and 2) don't confuse your balance sheet with accounting numbers that are not cash-pure.

In other words, when a company uses more cash and less stock to buy another company, investors can have greater confidence that future accounting numbers will reflect real cash values, not paper values. Here is what Buffett said about the mischief created by restructuring charges resulting from mergers:

> *In the acquisition arena, restructuring has been raised to an art form: Managements now frequently use mergers to dishonestly rearrange the value of assets and liabilities in ways that will allow them to both smooth and swell future earnings. Indeed, at deal*

time, major auditing firms sometimes point out the possibilities for a little accounting magic (or for a lot). Getting this push from the pulpit, first-class people will frequently stoop to third-class tactics. CEOs understandably do not find it easy to reject auditor-blessed strategies that lead to increased future "earnings."

Here's a true story that illustrates an all-too-common view in corporate America. The CEOs of two large banks, one of them a man who'd made many acquisitions, were involved not long ago in a friendly merger discussion (which in the end didn't produce a deal). The veteran acquirer was expounding on the merits of the possible combination, only to be skeptically interrupted by the other CEO: "But won't that mean a huge charge," he asked, "perhaps as much as $1 billion?" The "sophisticate" wasted no words: "We'll make it bigger than that – that's why we're doing the deal."

When you read a shareholder letter, it's prudent to note how active the company has been in buying and selling businesses. There's a good chance you'll find restructuring charges mentioned in the letter, but more likely in the footnotes. You'll want management to explain the nature of these charges. Without this knowledge, it is difficult to determine the gap between accounting earnings and cash.

The Cash Value of Businesses

Buffett's 2000 shareholder letter made three references to the importance of cash in valuing businesses.

First, he commented on the folly of putting money into "companies that have gigantic valuations relative to the cash they are likely to generate in the future." You may recall that in an earlier example his warning that this "heady experience" of seemingly effortless money "will eventually bring on pumpkins and mice."

Second, he cautioned investors that no one can ever "precisely predict the timing of cash flows in and out of a business or their exact amount." That is why Buffett and Munger try to keep their "estimates conservative and to focus on industries where business surprises are unlikely to wreak havoc on owners."

Finally, Buffett commented on the inadequacy of trying to come up with valuations for companies and other investments using "common yardsticks such as dividend yield, the ratio of price to earnings or to book value, and even growth rates [that] have *nothing* to do with valuation except to the extent they provide clues to the amount and timing of cash flows into and from the business."

Buffett chided investors who display ignorance, not sophistication, when they "glibly refer to 'growth' and 'value styles'" of investment. He thinks of growth and value as part of the same investment equation.

In fact, Buffett pointed out (as Enron learned the hard way) that growth at any cost will destroy value. This happens when large amounts of cash are required to start or continue business ventures that ultimately never produce enough cash to recover the cost of the investment, let alone generate additional profits.

Cash-Creating Potential: Intrinsic Value

Buffett approaches accounting like television's Jessica Fletcher tackled a murder mystery; but he is a financial sleuth. He wants to measure the gap between a company's accounting or GAAP earnings and its cash earnings.

He knows there will always be a gap because GAAP numbers can only approximate cash. He reminds investors that GAAP rules were created to help people count numbers, not to report the underlying value of the business. Figuring out this intrinsic business value is the job of investors. Buffett defines intrinsic value as the discounted cash flow of a business over its lifetime. That's why he zeroes in on cash. Buffett thinks about cash the way the King in the fairy tale Rumpelstiltskin thought about straw. The more high-quality straw you have, the more gold you can spin. When Buffett looks at a business, he wants to figure out the gold-producing potential of its straw/cash.

Chapter Eight

Sniffing Out Intrinsic Value:
Business Opportunities

OPPORTUNITY. *Date: 14th century*
1. a favorable juncture of circumstances
2. a good chance for advancement or progress
(Merriam-Webster Online Collegiate Dictionary)

You don't need to be a savvy accountant to get a "feel" for a company's intrinsic value. Remember that intrinsic value is simply the value of all the estimated future cash flows from a business. You'll learn more about this potential when you see how the CEO describes the company's **"business opportunities"** in the shareholder letter. As in the above definition, management and investors hope that the money invested in these opportunities will offer a good chance to advance the company's strategy. They hope it will result in more sales, higher revenues and ultimately sustain or increase the intrinsic value of the business.

It's pretty easy to spot descriptions of business activities in a shareholder letter. In 2000, all 100 companies in our survey reported on one or more business opportunities. Ford Motor Company had some of the strongest language in that year's survey. At one point, Ford directly connected its new product launches to its long-term strategic plan and the goal to reduce its dependence on North American earnings:

Opportunity to Grow Earnings Outside of North America
In 2000 we continued to be too dependent on North American earnings. With business conditions softening and competition getting more intense in the United States, correcting this imbalance becomes even more critical. We are implementing a long-term European Turnaround Strategy that is aggressive but achievable. That strategy includes the introduction of at least 45

new products in the next five years. We also have taken significant actions to improve our performance in South America.

Ford Motor also announced a new joint venture intended to increase revenues:

Wireless, Digital and Entertainment Services
Wingcast, our telematics joint venture with Qualcomm, was launched last year to bring wireless, digital information and entertainment services directly into our cars and trucks. Telematics services will be available in Europe this year, with a later debut in the United States.

They described other new products:

New Vehicle Lineup
In 2001, we will add to the strongest product lineup in our history with the launch of the new Ford Explorer, Thunderbird and Expedition in North America, and Ford Fiesta in Europe. Our new product launches also will include the new Lincoln Blackwood and Navigator, Land Rover Freelander and Range Rover, Jaguar X-Type, Aston Martin Vanquish, Mercury Mountaineer and Mazda Sport Wagon. These are exciting, segment-leading vehicles that will further distinguish us from our competition.

New and Expanded Business Opportunities

Shareholder letters describe two different kinds of business opportunities: activities that expand existing lines of business and activities that involve entering related or even unrelated businesses. In 2000, Buffett mentioned 14 business opportunities in his shareholder letter while Enron mentioned five. As you read the following excerpts, consider the respective degrees of willingness of Enron's and Berkshire's CEOs to disclose partner-friendly information.

EnronOnline

Here's what Enron said about EnronOnline, one of its new growth businesses:

In late 1999 we extended our successful business model to a web-based system, EnronOnline. EnronOnline has broadened our market reach, accelerated our business activity and enabled us to scale our business beyond our own expectations. By the end of 2000, EnronOnline had executed 548,000 transactions with a notional value of $336 billion, and it is now the world's largest web-based eCommerce system.

We're getting facts we can use to measure the success of EnronOnline: they've executed 548,000 transactions with a notional value of $336 billion. But what does this mean? What is "notional value"? Or put it this way: how much of this $336 billion of notional value could I take to the bank? It's not possible to estimate the intrinsic value of this business opportunity with these metrics. CEOs need to explain what they are doing with straight talk and in simple language if they want investors to fairly and accurately value their businesses.

What about Enron's assertion that it is "the world's largest web-based eCommerce system"? Without third-party validation, how can we verify this claim? Read on:

With EnronOnline, we are reaching a greater number of customers more quickly and at a lower cost than ever. It's a great new business generator, attracting users who are drawn by the site's ease of use, transparent, firm prices and the fact that they are transacting directly with Enron. In 2000 our total physical volumes increased significantly as a direct result of EnronOnline.

In this paragraph, we learn that EnronOnline's web-based system significantly increased total physical volumes. But what are "physical volumes"? Let's assume that the CEO had defined this term. Then I'd want to know how much the physical volumes had increased over a specific period of time. Otherwise, it's not possible to judge if management is spending its cash wisely.

Enron's description of Broadband Services provided details without telling why these were significant:

We have created a new market for bandwidth intermediation with Enron Broadband Services. In 2000 we completed 321 transactions with 45 counterparties. We are expanding our broadband intermediation capabilities to include a broad range of network services, such as dark fiber, circuits, Internet Protocol service and data storage. Our opportunities are increasing commensurately.

Part of the value we bring to the broadband field is network connectivity – providing the switches, the network intelligence and the intermediation skills to enable the efficient exchange of capacity between independent networks.

When I read the last sentence, I scratch my head and wonder again, what are they talking about?

Berkshire Hathaway: Investing in New Business Opportunities

Now let's look at Buffett's description of Berkshire Hathaway's new business opportunities in his 2000 shareholder letter. Remember that Buffett was busy acquiring eight businesses. One of these was Justin Industries:

In July we acquired Justin Industries, the leading maker of Western boots – including the Justin, Tony Lama, Nocona, and Chippewa brands – and the premier producer of brick in Texas and five neighboring states.

Here again, our acquisition involved serendipity. On May 4th, I received a fax from Mark Jones, a stranger to me, proposing that Berkshire join a group to acquire an unnamed company. I faxed him back, explaining that with rare exceptions we don't invest with others, but would happily pay him a commission if he sent details and we later made a purchase. He replied that the "mystery company" was Justin. I then went to Fort Worth to meet John Roach, chairman of the company and John Justin, who had built the business and was its major shareholder. Soon after, we bought Justin for $570 million in cash.

John Justin loved Justin Industries but had been forced to retire because of severe health problems (which sadly led to his death in late February). John was a class act – as a citizen, businessman and human being. Fortunately, he had groomed two outstanding managers, Harrold Melton at Acme and Randy Watson at Justin Boot, each of whom runs his company autonomously.

Acme, the larger of the two operations, produces more than one billion bricks per year at its 22 plants, about 11.7% of the industry's national output. The brick business, however, is necessarily regional, and in its territory Acme enjoys unquestioned leadership. When Texans are asked to name a brand of brick, 75% respond Acme, compared to 16% for the runner-up. (Before our purchase, I couldn't have named a brand of brick. Could you have?) This brand recognition is not only due to Acme's product quality, but also reflects many decades of extraordinary community service by both the company and John Justin.

I can't resist pointing out that Berkshire – whose top management has long been mired in the 19th century – is now one of the very few authentic "clicks-and-bricks" businesses around. We went into 2000 with GEICO doing significant business on the Internet, and then we added Acme. You can bet this move by Berkshire is making them sweat *in Silicon Valley.*

This is partner-friendly writing. In his shareholder letter, Buffett has willingly told us:

→ how the deal came about;

→ how much cash Berkshire paid;

→ how the company managed the transition after the founder's death;

→ the names of the new managers;

→ why Buffett has faith in the company's regional reputation,

→ why Acme's market share, brand recognition, quality of product and underlying competitive advantage made it attractive and;

→ how proud he was that Berkshire had become one of the only true "clicks-and-bricks" businesses.

Buffett does not disclose the cash flow potential of this acquisition, but neither would any other CEO. This is important competitive information. But we assume he followed the rule: buy businesses where the purchase price is startlingly low relative to the cash expected from the business over its lifetime. If Buffett applied this rule to valuing Justin and Acme, then we can reasonably assume that the cash paid to acquire these businesses was a fair and not an excessive price.

Investing in Ongoing Businesses

How did each company describe investments in its ongoing business? Here's what Enron wrote about the company's natural gas pipeline group, its bread-and-butter business:

> *The new name for our gas pipeline group accurately reflects a cultural shift to add more innovative customer services to our efficient pipeline operation. To serve our customers more effectively, we are increasingly incorporating the web into those relationships. Customers can go online to schedule nominations and handle inquiries, and they can transact for available capacity on EnronOnline. The pipelines continued to provide strong earnings and cash flow in 2000. Demand for natural gas is at a high in the United States, and we're adding capacity to take advantage of expansion opportunities in all markets. New capacity is supported by long-term contracts.*

This hard-asset business, which is regulated by the Federal Energy Regulatory Commission, earned respectable low double-digit earnings and provided stable cash flow. Changing the name of this business from the Enron Gas Pipeline Group to Enron Transportation Services shows the company's decision to focus on the service side of the business. Remember at that time, asset businesses were penalized by the stock market. The prices paid for service businesses were soaring.

Enron mentioned adding new capacity to take advantage of increased demand for natural gas, but it left out important details. We are left in the dark about:

→ How much capital is Enron investing to add capacity?

→ Where was Enron deciding to add capacity and what led to these decisions?

→ What is the outlook for earnings and cash flow for 2001 and beyond?

In contrast, read how excited Buffett is about the opportunities he sees ahead in Berkshire's aircraft services businesses: FlightSafety (FSI), a pilot-training business that he acquired in 1996 for $1.5 billion, and Executive Jet (EJA), a leader in fractional ownership of business jets that he acquired in 1998 for $725 million:

Al Ueltschi at FSI is now 83 and continues to operate at full throttle. Though I am not a fan of stock splits, I am planning to split Al's age 2-for-1 when he hits 100. (If it works, guess who's next.)

We spent $272 million on flight simulators in 2000, and we'll spend a similar amount this year. Anyone who thinks that the annual charges for depreciation don't reflect a real cost – every bit as real as payroll or raw materials – should get an internship at a simulator company. Every year we spend amounts equal to our depreciation charge simply to stay in the same economic place – and then spend additional sums to grow. And growth is in prospect for FSI as far as the eye can see.

Even faster growth awaits EJA (whose fractional-ownership program is called NetJets®). Rich Santulli is the dynamo behind this business.

Last year I told you that EJA's recurring revenue from monthly management fees and hourly usage grew by 46% in 1999. In 2000 the growth was 49%. I also told you that this was a low-margin business, in which survivors will be few. Margins were indeed slim at EJA last year, in part because of the major costs we are incurring in developing our business in Europe.

Regardless of the cost, you can be sure that EJA's spending on safety will be whatever is needed. Obviously, we would follow this policy under any circumstances, but there's some self-interest here as well: I, my wife, my children, my sisters, my 94-year-old aunt, all but one of our directors, and at least nine Berkshire managers regularly fly in the NetJets program. Given that cargo, I applaud Rich's insistence on unusually high amounts of pilot training (an average of 23 days a year). In addition, our pilots cement their skills by flying 800 or so hours a year. Finally, each flies only one model of aircraft, which means our crews do no switching around among planes with different cockpit and flight characteristics.

EJA's business continues to be constrained by the availability of new aircraft. Still, our customers will take delivery of more than 50 new jets in 2001, 7% of world output. We are confident we will remain the world leader in fractional ownership, in respect to number of planes flying, quality of service, and standards of safety.

In this excerpt, a number of important questions are answered that help us to appreciate the reasons for Buffett's enthusiasm. He tells us:

→ how much capital was spent and what it was spent on;

→ reminds readers that deprecation is a real expense and not just an accounting rule;

→ presents the year-to-year growth in revenues and;

→ offers a testimonial about how he and his family use EJA for their travel, thus hoping to increase sales.

Unlike Enron's letter, which does little to boost investor knowledge and confidence, the Berkshire Hathaway letter expresses business details in simple, but never simple-minded language.

But Buffett goes further in his shareholder letter than most CEOs. He not only describes his business investment opportunities, he wants us to understand how they will produce profits.

Chapter Nine

Drilling for Gushers:
Profit Drivers

PROFIT. *Etymology: Middle English, from Middle French, from Latin profectus, p.part. of proficere [to make progress, to profit]. Date: 14th century*
1. *an advantageous gain or return; benefit*
2. *the return on a business undertaking after all operating expenses have been met*
3. *the return on an investment after all charges have been paid; the rate of increase in the net worth of a business enterprise in a given accounting period; income from investments or property the amount received for a commodity or service in excess of the original cost*

(American Heritage College Dictionary, Third Edition)

Drilling for oil is expensive. When an oil rig burrows into Texas clay, developers pray they will find gushers, not dry holes. Similarly, CEOs want to invest in business opportunities that produce a steady flow of profits.

"Profit driver" language is an easy topic to spot in a shareholder letter. It is often signaled by terms like "profit," "profitable," "profitability" and "profit margins." These descriptions should reveal useful information about how a business opportunity will generate profits, how much profit to expect and how the profits will be used.

Profits are so important you'd think that every CEO letter would include profit driver language. But over one-third of the shareholder letters written for the year 2000 and analyzed in my annual survey didn't even include the word **"profit."**

Occasionally I spot insightful descriptions of profit drivers. Here's one example from the 2000 shareholder letter published by Jack in the Box, the fast-food restaurant chain:

Those who fret about the potentially negative impact of discounting, for instance, may not realize that while Jack in the Box offers a broad range of quality products with its value menu – a must-have in our industry – we also bolster our operating margins in a variety of ways. For example, we offer popular premium menu items and package them in combo meals and promotional groupings that are both attractive to guests and invaluable from a check-building stand-point. We have in-house commodities experts who have succeeded in keeping food costs as a percentage of sales down for the past several years. And our introduction of new technology in the kitchen, as mentioned earlier, promises to enhance efficiency in ways that can streamline operations and further support our growth.

Competitive Profit Margins

CEO Robert J. Nugent wastes no time dispelling investor skepticism about the company's ability to earn profits, or "operating margins." This term refers to the profits (margins) that result by subtracting all the direct costs of getting food to customers from the revenues produced by these efforts. Operating margins exclude taxes, interest expense and other indirect costs.

How can Jack in the Box bolster its slim margins in this intense competitive environment? First, they try to package meals in a way so that customers will pay a little more for their food ("check-building"); second, they hire special commodity experts who work to buy food at the lowest possible cost; and third, they invest in new technology that allows them to get more product and service for less cost. All these details build our awareness of the CEO's profit sensibility.

The Numbers Behind the Profits

Nugent's letter offers performance figures to illustrate the financial details of these initiatives:

Same-store average weekly sales, a key measure of success in the fast-food industry, grew 3.3 percent, a figure that's particularly impressive considering the company's 8.7 percent growth rate a year earlier. Same-store sales averages have now improved year-to-year for 23 consecutive quarters. And Jack in the Box was able to maintain its restaurant operating margins at 20 percent of sales –

no mean achievement, given that our 1999 operating margins benefited from a remarkable sales improvement driven by the implementation of our assemble-to-order, or "ATO," food-preparation systems. Meanwhile, system wide sales grew to $1.92 billion, or more than 11 percent over last year on a 52-week basis.

Reporting their same-store growth rates shows that the company is focused on profits that come from business operations. This growth rate excludes the sales that come from adding new stores. You won't find many companies that provide readers with detailed weekly and quarterly performance results. And you seldom find companies that tell you their restaurant operating margins. Most companies consider this sensitive data that could be used by competitors. In fact, armed with this data, you might well want to know the operating margins at McDonald's or Wendy's.

Indirect Costs and Profits

CEO Nugent also reports on the indirect costs of running Jack in the Box and how these affect company profits:

... general, administrative and other costs also remained about the same year-to-year, at 6.4 percent of revenues. We anticipate that these costs will trend downward over time, given that many of the initial infrastructure costs associated with opening our new southeastern markets have already been absorbed.

Few CEOs let you know in a shareholder letter that they are thinking about how general and indirect administrative costs compare to the company's revenues. Nugent isn't shy about disclosing this fact. He reminds investors that the costs associated with the company's expansion program in the southeast are being absorbed. This means that investors can expect to see an improvement in this relationship of indirect costs and revenues.

The Profit "Bottom Line"

Admitting that this may be more disclosure than a casual reader would want to know, the company provides an image that telegraphs the "bottom-line" significance of these results (emphasis added):

For those readers who may find that this blizzard of figures provides a more detailed portrait of our performance than they necessarily need, here's a snapshot that tells the story: <u>Jack in the Box was as profitable in the fourth quarter of fiscal 2000 as it was in the whole of fiscal year 1996</u>, and we're committed to an annual earnings-growth target of 15 percent.

Nugent tells you about the past, and then offers an insight into the future by announcing the company's annual earnings growth target. These details show investors why Jack in the Box's drilling expeditions are more likely to come up with gushers.

Enron and Profit Amnesia

In contrast to this informative report on fast-food profits, Enron's 2000 letter was disappointing. There was only one reference to a profit driver (emphasis added):

We recorded increasing positive earnings in all four quarters in 2000, and the business generated $103 million of recurring IBIT. Energy and facilities management outsourcing is now a proven concept, and we've established <u>a profitable deal flow</u>, which includes extensions of contracts by many existing customers.

Enron makes a Motherhood-like statement about profits – paying lip service to them, but offering no details. Enron fails to mention the factors that produce this "profitable deal flow."

In my review of Enron's annual shareholder letters written from 1996 to 2000, I found the word "profit" or other profit-like words only six times. In my review of Berkshire Hathaway letters written during this same time period, I found 90 uses of the root word "profit" and related terms.

A Smorgasbord of Profit Drivers

Buffett's 2000 letter is a smorgasbord of profit margins and drivers. Read his letter and you will find seven different ways he thinks about profits at Berkshire Hathaway:

Profits and Pricing Policies

CEOs show off their profit sensibility when they tell you how management is focused on pricing the company's products and services to maximize profits. Here's what Buffett said about the pricing policies at General Re, their large reinsurance company (emphasis added):

> *At General Re, the news has turned considerably better: Ron Ferguson, along with Joe Brandon, Tad Montross, and a talented supporting cast took many actions <u>during 2000 to bring that company's profitability back to past standards. Though our pricing is not fully corrected, we have significantly repriced business that was severely unprofitable or dropped it altogether</u>.*

In describing the company's profitability as below standard due to pricing practices, he warns us about potential problems at General Re. He acknowledges the team's efforts to reprice policies to meet profit standards. (Apparently, they did not work fast enough: a new team was announced in Buffett's Third Quarter 2001 letter.)

Profits and Cost Control

A CEO who writes about keeping costs under control builds investor trust in his or her ability to turn a profit. Cost-control consciousness is not as common as one might expect in shareholder letters. Only one-third of the companies in our 2000 shareholder letter survey mentioned cost-cutting initiatives. Here's what Buffett said about GEICO's approach (emphasis added):

> *GEICO will be a huge part of Berkshire's future. Because of its rock-bottom operating costs, it offers a great many Americans the cheapest way to purchase a high-ticket product that they <u>must</u> buy. The company then couples this bargain with service that consistently ranks high in independent surveys. <u>That's a combination inevitably producing growth and profitability.</u>*

Profit Margins and Competitive Advantage

Companies that pay attention to profit margins gain a leg up on the competition. Here's what Buffett said about ExecuJet's margins (emphasis added):

> *Last year I told you that EJA's recurring revenue from monthly management fees and hourly usage grew by 46% in 1999. In 2000 the growth was 49%. <u>I also told you that this was a low-margin</u>*

business, in which survivors will be few. Margins were indeed slim at EJA last year, in part because of the major costs we are incurring in developing our business in Europe.

Few CEOs tell you if they are in a high or low margin business. It's useful information. Buffett treats readers like insiders by revealing what makes this a tough business. Like CEO Nugent, he acknowledges the costs associated with expanding the business. Buffett shows that he trusts readers with sensitive information about business risk – he tells us that ExecuJet's growth in Europe is weakening already slim margins, Paradoxically, these insights build rather than weaken CEO credibility.

Profit Expectations
Buffett even provided the profit expectations for his insurance business:

We're pleased by the growth in our float during 2000 but not happy with its cost. Over the years, our cost of float has been very close to zero, with the underwriting profits realized in most years offsetting the occasional terrible year such as 1984, when our cost was a staggering 19%. In 2000, however, we had an underwriting loss of $1.6 billion, which gave us a float cost of 6%. Absent a mega-catastrophe, we expect our float cost to fall in 2001 – perhaps substantially – in large part because of corrections in pricing at General Re that should increasingly be felt as the year progresses. On a smaller scale, GEICO may experience the same improving trend.

Each year, Buffett offers a lengthy discussion explaining the terms "underwriting profits" and "float," so readers can appreciate how Berkshire Hathaway makes money. (I will attempt a brief explanation, but encourage readers to look on pages 8-9 in his 2000 shareholder letter for a definitive explanation.)

Making "underwriting profits" is the goal of all insurance businesses. These profits result from properly identifying and pricing risks and from managing the insurance premium income. "Insurance float" is a key concept to understanding how insurance companies make money. This "float" is created when companies receive premiums paid by their customers. The company gets to invest this cash or "float" until it must pay out for claims. An underwriting profit is recorded when the company earns investment returns that are greater than the cost of paying claimants' losses.

Buffett notes that Berkshire's cost of float could fall substantially due to re-pricing General Re's business – provided there were no mega-catastrophes in 2001 that required a payout of huge sums. The September 11th attacks dashed these hopes. In the third quarter 2001, Berkshire announced it would take an estimated $3.0 billion write-off to pay claims associated with the attacks.

Did this announcement cause the stock to decline? As you may recall, Berkshire stock dropped in price as did many other company stocks after the terrorist attacks. But it rebounded to its pre-September 11th price only two weeks later. Over the years, Buffett and Munger have warned their investors to expect lumpy earnings. While the nature of this loss had never been contemplated, the loss itself had been anticipated. Berkshire is managed for the long term.

Praise for Profits

Buffett sets himself apart from most CEOs when he gives his managers the credit for creating profits (emphasis added):

> <u>*In aggregate, our smaller insurance operations produced an excellent underwriting profit in 2000*</u> *while generating significant float – just as they have done for more than a decade. If these companies were a single and separate operation, people would consider it an outstanding insurer. Because the companies instead reside in an enterprise as large as Berkshire, the world may not appreciate their accomplishments – but I sure do. Last year I thanked Rod Eldred, John Kizer, Don Towle and Don Wurster, and I again do so. In addition, we now also owe thanks to Tom Nerney at U.S. Liability and Michael Stearns, the new head of Cypress.*

In my 100-company survey in 2000, only six other companies thanked their managers. Of these, no other company that we surveyed in 2000 directly credited its management for producing profits. You can bet that investors and also the other Berkshire managers took note of this praise.

Profits and Compensation

Profits can be used to motivate employees. CEOs link them with incentive compensation: the greater the company's year-end profits, the more employees get paid. Here's what Buffett wrote about auto insurer GEICO's profit-sharing practice:

> *I've told you about our profit-sharing arrangement at GEICO that targets only two variables – growth in policies and the underwriting results of seasoned business. Despite the headwinds of 2000, we still had a performance that produced an 8.8% profit-sharing payment, amounting to $40.7 million.*

Buffett prefers to reward employees for creating profits, rather than increasing the company stock price. Elsewhere in the letter, he states that he'd rather keep the players focused on the playing field; he'll keep track of the scoreboard.

Profits and Tax Policies

Tax policies affect corporate profits. This can be a significant expense, so it's valuable to consider how it impacts profits and, ultimately, intrinsic value. But few CEOs mention this connection in their shareholder letters.

Buffett does. Here's how he described this impact in his 2000 shareholder letter:

> *The tax code makes Berkshire's owning 80% or more of a business far more profitable for us, proportionately, than our owning a smaller share. When a company we own all of earns $1 million after tax, the entire amount inures to our benefit. If the $1 million is upstreamed to Berkshire, we owe no tax on the dividend. And, if the earnings are retained and we were to sell the subsidiary – not likely at Berkshire! – for $1 million more than we paid for it, we would owe no capital gains tax. That's because our "tax cost" upon sale would include both what we paid for the business and all earnings it subsequently retained.*

> *Contrast that situation to what happens when we own an investment in a marketable security. There, if we own a 10% stake*

in a business earning $10 million after tax, our $1 million share of the earnings is subject to additional state and federal taxes of (1) about $140,000 if it is distributed to us (our tax rate on most dividends is 14%); or (2) no less than $350,000 if the $1 million is retained and subsequently captured by us in the form of a capital gain (on which our tax rate is usually about 35%, though it sometimes approaches 40%). We may defer paying the $350,000 by not immediately realizing our gain, but eventually we must pay the tax. In effect, the government is our "partner" twice when we own part of a business through a stock investment, but only once when we own at least 80%.

Don't expect other CEOs to describe the government as their partner. And don't expect this level of detailed analysis. In 1998, Buffett added a description to show Berkshire's largesse to the government. It was a shareholder letter first – a CEO who boasts about paying taxes:

The federal income taxes that Berkshire and General Re have paid, or will soon pay, in respect to 1998 earnings total $2.7 billion. That means we shouldered all of the U.S. Government's expenses for more than a half-day.

Follow that thought a little further: If only 625 other U.S. taxpayers had paid the Treasury as much as we and General Re did last year, no one else – neither corporations nor 270 million citizens – would have had to pay federal income taxes or any other kind of federal tax (for example, social security or estate taxes). Our shareholders can truly say that they "gave at the office."

Buffett's ability to turn subjects as potentially numbing as taxes into mini-dramas with action, protagonists, and emotion makes his CEO letters distinctive.

Looking for stories in CEO shareholder letters is an important part of my analysis of shareholder letters. Find a good shareholder letter story and you can judge if the CEO is able to realize the benefits of having two brains, not one.

Chapter Ten

Two Brains Are Better Than One:

CEO Stories

STORY. *Etymology: Middle English storie, [story], from Old French estorie, estoire, from Latin historia. Date: 13th century*
1. *an account or a recital of an event or series of events*
2. *a usually fictional narrative intended to interest or amuse the hearer or reader; a tale*
3. *a short story*
4. *an incident, experience, or subject that furnishes or would be interesting material for a narrative*
5. *the plot of a narrative or dramatic work*
6. *a report, a statement, or an allegation of facts*
7. *a news article or broadcast; the event, situation, or other material for a widely circulated rumor*
(American Heritage College Dictionary, Third Edition)

Our brain has two parts: the right side and the left side. Our left side-brain manages our intellectual, analytic, and reasoning skills, which are often called our "masculine" abilities. The right side-brain manages our imaginative, intuitive, and emotional intelligence skills. These are described as "feminine" qualities.

CEOs who use both sides of their brains are better equipped to manage and lead a business in today's super-charged environment. These CEOs can make quick critical decisions even when they are unable to gather all the important facts. They use their powers of reasoning and intuition to transform facts and perceptions into knowledge and wisdom. But how can an investor judge if a CEO is fully utilizing both sides of his or her brain? I look for **"stories"** in shareholder letters that communicate facts and emotional truths.

Eighty-three percent of the companies in our 2000 survey included such stories in their CEO shareholder letters. Many of these vividly demonstrated the CEO's character and competence. But few CEO stories were as meaningful as Buffett's narratives. In the following example, Buffett draws on analysis and intuition to explain his decision to acquire the Ben Bridge Jeweler chain in 2000:

The Acquisition of Ben Bridge Jeweler

Ben Bridge Jeweler was another purchase we made by phone, prior to any face-to-face meeting between me and the management. Ed Bridge, who with his cousin, Jon, manages this 65-store West Coast retailer, is a friend of Barnett Helzberg, from whom we bought Helzberg Diamonds in 1995. Upon learning that the Bridge family proposed to sell its company, Barnett gave Berkshire a strong recommendation. Ed then called and explained his business to me, also sending some figures, and we made a deal, again half for cash and half for stock.

Ed and Jon are fourth generation owner-managers of a business started 89 years ago in Seattle. Both the business and the family – including Herb and Bob, the fathers of Jon and Ed – enjoy extraordinary reputations. Same-store sales have increased by 9%, 11%, 13%, 10%, 12%, 21% and 7% over the past seven years, a truly remarkable record.

It was vital to the family that the company operate in the future as in the past. No one wanted another jewelry chain to come in and decimate the organization with ideas about synergy and cost saving (which, though they would never work, were certain to be tried). I told Ed and Jon that they would be in charge, and they knew I could be believed: After all, it's obvious that your Chairman would be a disaster at actually running a store or selling jewelry (though there are members of his family who have earned black belts as purchasers).

In their typically classy way, the Bridges allocated a substantial portion of the proceeds from their sale to the hundreds of co-workers who had helped the company achieve its success. We're proud to be associated with both the family and the company.

Look at the reasons why Buffett acquired Ben Bridge Jeweler. First, he is impressed with the 89-year-old-firm's solid reputation. A company's reputation is so important that some CEOs will try to manufacture it through expensive advertising and marketing campaigns. They call it strengthening the "brand image."

Buffett doesn't do this. He insists that a company's reputation can never be bought. The company's reputation is linked to the time-tested quality of its products and services. Brand image is strengthened daily by the actions of people who stand behind company promises. This belief is the focus of Buffett's comments.

He also examines the impressive growth of Ben Bridge's same-store sales. This shows how the company's management distinguishes between the growth from operations improvements and the addition of new stores. This awareness reveals a business with a strong profit focus.

Buffett gives equal time to business principles. He admires the former owners of Ben Bridge Jeweler for not wanting to auction off their business to a jewelry chain that might tarnish the company's already shining reputation. He notes with pride that Ed and Jon Bridge gave their employees a substantial part of the profits after selling to Berkshire.

Buffett includes principled business behavior in his shopping list when he's looking for businesses to buy. We look for this same kind of behavior in CEO shareholder letters. It's usually the mark of a business with staying power.

Four Different Types of CEO Stories

Over the years, I have discovered four different types of stories inside shareholder letters. Each type illustrates a different kind of left-brain and right-brain ability:

1. **Joe Friday, Just the Facts Stories**: Gathering and reporting facts in a chronological order.

2. **Connect the Dots Stories**: Presenting facts in a context that reveals the underlying business strategy and motivations.

3. **You've Gotta Have Heart Stories**: Using imagination to describe facts so that they touch the reader's head and heart.

4. **Wise Words and Parables**: Telling a story so that it reveals fundamental values and imparts wisdom.

The first two examples demonstrate predominately left-brain abilities. The last two examples demonstrate both right *and* left-brain abilities.

Look at the first example of story telling.

Sgt. Joe Friday, Just the Fact Stories

The kinds of stories we find most frequently in CEO shareholder letters are chronologies. I call these Sgt. Joe Friday stories. Police detective Joe Friday was the star of the early television show, *Dragnet*. Each week in a voice stripped of emotion, Friday would ask crime victims, "Tell me what happened Ma'am, just the facts." He wanted accounts that stuck to the facts and ignored emotions and interpretations.

When facts are presented as a chronology with a beginning, middle and end, but without much embellishment, you've found a Sgt. Joe Friday story. Here's an example from the 2000 shareholder letter of insurance giant AIG (American Insurance Group):

AIG: Getting Licensed in Vietnam

As reported last year, early in 2000 American International Assurance Company, Ltd. [AIA] [a subsidiary of the company] *received a life insurance license from the government of Vietnam to operate a wholly owned life company in that country, the first insurance license granted by Vietnam to a U.S.-based company. Our new Hanoi and Ho Chi Minh City offices opened in October. We now have an agency force of approximately 1,800 and the new company is achieving faster growth than its original business plan.*

This story highlights the following facts: AIG was the first U.S.-based company to be granted an insurance license by the government of Vietnam; it employs 1,800 people; and it is growing faster than anticipated. We get information, but we're not given a context in which to appreciate its significance. We are not told how this fits into AIG's overall strategy. It's not the kind of story you would be likely to retell to your friends.

Another Just the Facts example comes from Wells Fargo's 2000 shareholder letter:

Wells Fargo: Integrating the Merger

I believe ours was the largest and most complex systems conversion in banking history. In 2000 alone, we had 63 separate conversions, more than one a weekend. These conversions connected what now is America's most extensive banking franchise – 23 Midwestern and Western states spanning more than 3,000 miles across five time zones from Van Wert, Ohio, to Bethel, Alaska. The conversions affected more than 14 million banking customers, 2,900 banking stores and 6,500 ATMs. The result is we now present ourselves as one brand to our customers. They can save more time and money than ever before and benefit from the convenience of one of North America's largest and most diversified financial services companies.

In this story, CEO Richard Kovacevich, effectively helps us to understand an important element of Wells Fargo's business. The reference to the far-flung cities served by the bank creates a memorable image about the size and scope of its merger with Norwest Bank and how they expect to serve customers. Still, it's not the type of tale one is likely to retell.

What about CEO stories that fail? Try to understand Advanced Micro Devices' 2000 shareholder letter:

AMD: Introducing the Hammer Family

Looking beyond the current year, in the first half of 2002, we plan to introduce the Hammer Family and 64-bit computing to our markets. The Hammer Family is the culmination of our long-term strategy for a totally independent alternative that will extend our lead in PC processors and provide competitive platform solutions for PC servers and workstations.

Innovation is all about ideas, and the Hammer Family is clearly a better idea.

The AMD x86-64 technology will deliver unsurpassed 32-bit performance in Windows computing while enabling a seamless transition to 64-bit computing.

Our eighth-generation Hammer Family will be manufactured in the next-generation 130-nanometer, HiP-7 technology, again co-developed through our Motorola alliance. All versions of the

Hammer Family will employ SOI (silicon-on-insulator) technology for enhanced performance and reduced power consumption. As yet another example of our virtual gorilla strategy, we have entered into an agreement with IBM, the industry leader in SOI technology, relating to the design of SOI devices to enhance the success of the Hammer Family.

AMD innovations in the instruction set, I/O capability, and architecture in our eighth-generation Hammer Family are designed to catapult AMD to leadership in a 64-bit world in our third 1,000 days.

That's a story for next year's letter.

It's clear that AMD's CEO wants to tell a story, but technical jargon gets in his way. Their "virtual gorilla strategy" is catchy-sounding, but it's hard to grasp the basic facts well enough to get a picture of their battle plan. Without these, it's not possible to discern the CEO's strategic sense.

Chapter Eleven

Show and Tell Me:

Strategic Sense

SENSE. *Etymology: Middle English [meaning], from Old French sens, from Latin sensus, [the faculty of perceiving]; p.part. of sentire [to feel]*
1. *any of the faculties by which stimuli are received and felt, as the faculties of hearing, sight, and equilibrium*
2. *intuitive or acquired perception or ability to estimate; a capacity to appreciate or understand*
3. *normal ability to think or reason soundly; correct judgment; something sound or reasonable*
4. *judgment; consensus; intellectual interpretation*
> *(American Heritage College Dictionary, Third Edition)*

The topic that is most frequently cited in a shareholder letter is **"corporate strategy."** No surprise here. When we learn about a company's plans to make money from tangible assets, like plant and equipment, and intangible assets, such as patents, brand recognition and new technology – we get to the heart and soul of financial analysis. Here is how Procter and Gamble described its strategy in the 2000 shareholder letter (emphasis added):

> *We have learned a lot from our experience over the past year, and have applied this learning to a four-point plan to drive both sales and profit growth.*

> *First, we are focusing sharply on building our biggest, strongest global brands, the core of our business. We need to be sure we are consistently growing our market share on these brands.*

> *Second, we are making tougher choices about investing in new products and new businesses. We'll use fast-cycle learning techniques to get rapid consumer validation of our biggest ideas, and commercialize those ideas more quickly worldwide.*

> *Third, we are working hard to get even more value from our strong customer relationships. We'll build on this strength by*

collaborating more closely with customers. The result will be even more innovative marketing programs for new and established brands alike.

Fourth, we are placing greater emphasis on rigorous cost control and cash management. We deployed teams to drive out waste and to find new efficiencies in overhead management, marketing support and product costs. In addition, we've renewed our emphasis on capital investment and working-capital efficiency.

Many companies describe the corporate strategy as a list of action steps they intend to take. But such a list only tells you what a CEO plans to do. They don't show how these steps are being acted out in real-life situations. That's why I give CEOs extra credit when they describe strategic stories. These shareholder letter stories give readers a feel for the CEO's **"strategic sense."**

The word "sense," as indicated on the previous page, has multiple meanings. I particularly like the reference to common sense, but others are equally important. It can also apply to intuition and the capacities to appreciate and to judge. Stories that reveal a CEO's strategic sense add shading, depth and significance to corporate plans. They show and tell you about the corporate strategy. This story from transportation giant CSX's 1999 shareholder letter offers insights into its decision to sell part of the international shipping business:

CSX: What Hasn't Changed

Selling Sea-Land's international business was a hard but necessary decision. Since its founding in 1956, Sea-Land has been a great company, an unquestioned industry leader and innovator. The company introduced the containerization concept to global shipping, revolutionizing the way goods move around the world. Since being acquired by CSX in 1986, Sea-Land revenues tripled, and the company established strong market positions in virtually all of the world's major trade routes. Over the years, its talented management team, led by John Clancey, has contributed much to our company, and we are fortunate to have retained a number of key executives.

But recent years have seen profit margins decline as a number of strong, well-capitalized competitors entered this business. Projected worldwide vessel over-capacity and substantial, ongoing capital requirements pointed to a worrisome outlook, and we made the strategic decision to sell Sea-Land's international business assets to Danish carrier, Maersk Line. This transaction was completed in December 1999, generating net cash proceeds of approximately $750 million and transferring substantial vessel lease obligations to the buyer.

We have retained those parts of the business that currently earn their costs of capital and have more certain futures. The newly formed CSX Lines, engaged in Jones Act-protected domestic shipping, and CSX World Terminals, which operates container terminals in Hong Kong and nine other overseas locations, are now independent business units. Headed by former Sea-Land senior executives Chuck Raymond and Bob Grassi, respectively, and supported by strong management teams, these companies will grow, and we are optimistic about their prospects.

Importantly, the Sea-Land sale strengthens our financial position and eliminates a large degree of uncertainty that has adversely affected investor valuations of CSX. The transaction is a "win/win" for CSX and Maersk. Sea-Land international assets are in strong, familiar hands, and we are confident that the combined company will emerge as the clear leader in the international container-shipping industry. Looking forward, our strategic emphasis is overwhelmingly rail-oriented, and we are focusing sharply on maximizing the benefits of the Conrail transaction.

In this example, we learn about the profitability and competitive challenges of international shipping. We get to see how management analyzes the problems facing this business:

→ *The Situation:* CSX had been a leader in the worldwide container-shipping business. New financially strong competitors were challenging its ability to make profits. CSX didn't expect this situation to improve soon.

→ *The Solution:* Keeping the parts of its business that were financially strong, CSX sold the underperforming business to Maersk Line.

→ *The Outlook:* Financially strengthened from the cash proceeds of the sale, CSX now intends to focus on its railroad business in order to realize the benefits of the Conrail acquisition.

When CEOs offer strategic stories we get to see how they combine the pieces that make up their corporate strategy. An unintended benefit is that when information is presented this way, we get a clearer picture of pieces that have been omitted. For example, in Reebok's 2000 shareholder letter, the company enthusiastically announced a deal to become the exclusive franchisee for the National Football League:

Reebok: NFL Partnership

The newest member of our Reebok family is the NFL Brand. In December 2000, Reebok and the NFL sealed what is arguably the most comprehensive deal ever recorded in the history of the sports industry. Beginning with the 2002 season we will obtain a ten year exclusive license to manufacture, market and sell NFL licensed merchandise in our key trade channels of distribution. These channels include athletic specialty, sporting goods and better department stores. Additionally, the NFL has granted Reebok the exclusive rights to design and distribute all NFL replica jerseys, headwear, footwear and gloves for all channels of distribution. This unprecedented partnership represents a strategic alliance between two of the most powerful and recognizable sports brands in the world and we believe this alliance will generate long-term profitability and sales growth for both Reebok and the NFL.

In this story, CEO Paul B. Fireman offers some interesting details so readers can appreciate why this deal makes sense: Reebok's exclusive agreement with the NFL will last for ten years; Reebok will sell both clothing and sporting goods in many different kinds of stores and outlets; and Reebok expects this alliance to grow both profits and sales.

This is impressive, but the information raises additional questions. Beyond the obvious goal of making more money, we don't see why Reebok chose this strategy over others. How was Reebok able to beat out rivals, such as Nike, and get this exclusive agreement? How much did the agreement cost Reebok and how does that cost compare to other similar franchise agreements? Why is the NFL a more natural alliance for Reebok than another sport might be? We can assume that Reebok's CEO considered these questions, but his shareholder letter does not offer evidence to confirm this belief.

The next story, from Boise Cascade's 2000 shareholder letter, also offers important strategic information:

Boise Cascade: Forest Stewardship Program

In 1999, we expanded our internal Forest Stewardship Program to include a more comprehensive set of forest management objectives. Compliance with our own Forest Stewardship Values and Measures and the SFI standard is incorporated into all our forest management plans and programs. To provide independent assurance of compliance with the SFI standard, Boise Cascade retained PricewaterhouseCoopers LLP, an international audit firm, to conduct a series of third-party audits of our forest management practices.

PricewaterhouseCoopers had completed two of our scheduled audits, covering approximately 500,000 acres, at year-end. We are pleased to report that Boise Cascade's forest management and standing timber purchase programs in the Western Oregon and Idaho Regions were found to meet the SFI standard. These forest management audits will be extended to all our lands in 2001 and then will be ongoing, with audits repeated every three years. As part of the audit program, Boise Cascade customers are invited to accompany the audit teams into the forests to observe their work.

We learn surprising facts about the forest products industry in this story. Did you know that such companies had established "Forest Stewardship Values and Measures" and retained accounting firms to conduct audits of its forest management practices? I didn't know this. But this new information leads me to several unanswered questions: Why is Boise Cascade conducting these audits and what do they cost? Was the company required to set up these audits, or are they an industry-wide practice? How will this practice help Boise Cascade win in its business? How do customers benefit from joining the audit teams? Answers to these questions would have shed more light on Boise Cascade's pursuit of profits and principles.

What About Enron?

Enron was an undisputed innovator when it came to opening up new natural gas trading markets, but how was this revealed in its strategic stories? It's difficult to tell. Particularly between 1998 and 2000, Enron's stories lacked straight talk and plain facts. For example, none of the stories in its 2000 letter would have satisfied Sgt. Joe Friday. Without such a factual basis, CEO letters fail to inform, teach, and cannot confidently be relied upon to make decisions.

A passage from Enron's 2000 letter illustrates this problem:

Enron's Competitive Advantages

Our size, experience and skills give us enormous competitive advantages. We have:

→ *Robust networks of strategic assets that we own or have contractual access to, which give us greater flexibility and speed to reliably deliver widespread logistical solutions.*

→ *Unparalleled liquidity and market-making abilities that result in price and service advantages.*

→ *Risk management skills that enable us to offer reliable prices as well as reliable delivery.*

→ *Innovative technology such as EnronOnline to deliver products and services easily at the lowest possible cost.*

These capabilities enable us to provide high-value products and services other wholesale service providers cannot. We can take the physical components and repackage them to suit the specific needs of customers. We treat term, price and delivery as variables that are blended into a single, comprehensive solution. Our technology and fulfillment systems ensure execution. In current market environments, these abilities make Enron the right company with the right model at the right time.

This story raises more important questions than those raised by the Reebok and Boise Cascade stories. We're not even sure what Enron is talking about. For instance, what are these "robust networks of strategic assets" that allow the company to "deliver widespread logistical solutions"? If a general in battle talked this way, I doubt that his army would have known in which direction to march. While energy industry insiders are familiar with terms like, "liquidity and market-making abilities," "risk management skills," and "innovative technology," most other readers would rightly feel that Enron wasn't interested in helping shareholders to understand its business.

Enron hasn't told us what makes its strategy different. All energy trading companies treat "term, price and delivery as variables that are blended into a single, comprehensive solution." How do these abilities give Enron a competitive edge? Furthermore, the statement that "our technology and fulfillment systems ensure execution" sounds silly. It implies that people are irrelevant in its strategic equation. According to this notion, systems, not people, ensure execution. Enron weakly ends the story with a cliché, "the right company at the right time."

Enron's 1999 Stories: Sleight of Hand

The following story from Enron's 1999 letter offers a clearer picture of the company's strategy. It described plans to replicate the lessons learned in creating a national energy trading market to develop markets in new fast-growing industries, like broadband (emphasis added):

Enron: Extending our Skills and Experience
Enron's entry into the communications business is a logical extension of our skills and experience. The industry is strikingly similar to the natural gas industry of the mid-1980s. At that time, Enron remade an industry characterized by inflexible and rigid business relationships and contracts, which caused either crippling shortages or massive inefficiencies. Enron challenged conventional thinking and helped open the industry for effective competition.

We have the capacity to develop a similar efficient market for bandwidth.

As EnronOnline demonstrates, the Internet is changing the way we do business. The public Internet, however, does not have sufficient bandwidth capacity to carry massive data and rich media content to the desktop. In 1999 we rolled out Enron Broadband Services to take the Internet to the next level. <u>Demand for premium broadband delivery services is expected to soar by 150 percent annually from now through 2004. This market could easily surpass the combined markets for natural gas and electricity.</u>

Enron Broadband Services is off to a tremendous start: we own and operate a superior intelligent fiber optic network that is focused on delivering bandwidth-intensive content, such as TV-quality video, over the Internet. <u>Our goal is to be the premier provider of high-bandwidth services and applications worldwide. The business model we follow is the one we used to create liquid markets for natural gas and electricity. We are establishing benchmark bandwidth contracts and making a market in bandwidth. We initiated the first bandwidth trade in December 1999. The market for bandwidth intermediation will grow from $30 billion in 2000 to $95 billion in 2004. With our head start, we expect to become the leader in this field.</u>

This story illustrates Enron's skillful use of the magician's sleight of hand. As evidenced by all the underlining in the above story, readers are drawn to images of markets where growth is explosive and always trending upward. Conveniently, these visions distract us from Enron's present challenge – its need to replicate its success in creating an energy-trading market to service the new broadband services industry.

In order to understand how Enron will succeed in pulling off this strategy, we need to be able to compare these two businesses. But Enron never gives us enough information to do so. In fact, Enron's characterization of the natural gas industry as "the inflexible and rigid business relationships and contracts, which caused either crippling shortages or massive inefficiencies" describes an industry that has little in common with the dynamic broadband industry. The hallmarks of this industry are highly fluid and constantly evolving business relationships and contracts.

More insights about Enron's strategic sense were revealed in the following passage, also from the 1999 letter (emphasis added):

> By structuring our operations as flexible networks, we can accelerate our growth with minimal capital expenditures. _Physical assets play a strategic_, but not central, role in the way we earn our money, and this reduced emphasis on merely earning a return on _physical assets allows us to divest non-strategic assets_ and redeploy capital into higher-growth and stronger-return businesses. This led to several important transactions last year.

They use the word "strategic" to suggest that physical assets are not central to the way they earn money. (This was particularly true for dot.com businesses at that time.) The remark about the company's "reduced emphasis on merely earning a return on physical assets" seems unnecessary. Isn't a company better off when it can make money from both physical and non-physical assets?

One transaction that would have allowed Enron to redeploy capital into "higher growth businesses" was the company's decision to sell Portland General Electric, an electric utility headquartered in Portland, Oregon. In this story, we are unexpectedly reminded about the importance of cash:

Enron: Selling Portland General
In November, we agreed to sell Portland General Electric (PGE) to Sierra Pacific Resources. PGE is an excellent organization, and our relationship has been mutually beneficial. At the time we acquired PGE, Enron needed additional insight into developing electricity markets, and we also required credibility to participate in the markets. We have gained the insight and credibility we sought, and we believe the sale of PGE represents the best value to Enron shareholders. After the sale, we will have approximately $2 billion in cash proceeds to redeploy into businesses with faster growth and higher returns. The agreement is currently under regulatory review, with a final sale expected in late 2000.

But Enron never completed its sale of Portland General. (Although, it neglected to mention this fact in its next year's shareholder letter.) By the end of 2001, the employees of Portland General, just like their Enron colleagues, lost everything they had invested in the company. In hindsight, we might well wonder why these employees could not have seen what was apparent in these letters: Enron operated in a world of strategic illusion, not strategic sense. Relying on illusion is always a risky business.

Chapter Twelve:

Emotional Advantage:
Imagination and Feelings

EMOTION. *Etymology: Old French esmovoir, from Latin emovEre [to move]. Date: 1579*
1. *an intense mental state that arises subjectively rather than through conscious effort; a strong feeling*
2. *a state of mental agitation or disturbance*
3. *the part of the consciousness that involves feeling; sensibility*
                    (American Heritage College Dictionary, Third Edition)

The strategic stories in the last chapter may engage our heads, but they do not touch our hearts. Stories that connect with our heads and hearts tap into right *and* left-brain ways of knowing. These stories reveal the imagination and feelings that CEOs bring to their corporate plans, actions and results. We get to glimpse the CEO's heart and soul, or, as more cynical readers might say, the lack of these qualities.

In the not-too-distant past, most workplaces were treated as emotion-free zones. Even if emotions were recognized, they were not welcomed. It was a sign of weakness to express one's feelings. Executives and human resources experts regarded emotions (the physical experience of feelings) and feelings (the way we interpret events) as roadblocks to progress. Messy and difficult-to-manage emotions were particularly unwelcome. It's hard to meet productivity and efficiency goals when employees *act out*.

But times have changed. Emotions are now regarded as a key factor in corporate performance. Experts administer EQ tests to measure emotional intelligence. They recognize both the positive and negative contributions of emotions and feelings. These new-age emotional advisors believe that companies can gain an emotional advantage when they tap into the **"imagination and feelings"** of their constituents.

Stock Prices and Emotions

In each year's survey, I analyze the emotional content in shareholder letters. First, I highlight commonplace emotional words like "excited," "proud" and "confident" and less common words like "love," "fun" and "frustrated." Over the past three years, I found that 15 percent of the letters in the survey are entirely devoid of emotional words such as these.

What about the other 85 percent? Over half of these letters fail to present emotional words in a way that conveys emotion to readers. For example, John Eyler, Jr., the new CEO of Toys "R" Us, wrote this passage in his 2000 letter:

> *Ours is a company ripe with opportunity. Everywhere we look, we see opportunities to grow our business, and it's no exaggeration to say that I'm even more excited and energized about the Toys "R" Us organization now than I was when I first joined the company in January, 2000.*

He describes emotion, but he doesn't *create* emotion. The passage is neither exciting nor energizing. In contrast, here's how Michael Eisner, the Chairman and CEO of The Walt Disney Company, described his view of the company's potential:

> ### Disney: Accelerating on Many, but Not All Cylinders
> *As strong as this year was, it really was the equivalent of a race car accelerating nicely on many, but not all, of its cylinders. Let me borrow one of our new Autopia cars to illustrate what I mean.*
>
> *During the year, one of the improvements we made at Disneyland, working with our colleagues at Chevron, was to update Autopia with these new, more environment-friendly vehicles. But, for purposes of this letter, this car can symbolize our company, and here's how it looks under the hood.*
>
> *The Disney corporate engine is powered by five cylinders: Media Networks, Parks and Resorts, Consumer Products, Studio Entertainment and the Walt Disney Internet Group.*
>
> *Throughout much of the '90s, we were truly firing on all cylinders (of course, we didn't have as many as we have now), and the company kept posting solid double-digit growth. What I found most remarkable about 2000 was that our robust growth was*

achieved with just two of the cylinders firing at 100 percent. I find it very exciting to ponder what this vehicle can achieve when all five cylinders are fully and harmoniously functioning at peak performance.

This passage has emotional and imaginative power. We're asked to think about Disney as a racecar engine "firing on many cylinders," even during a year of mixed performance. We learn that two of the five cylinders are operating at 100 percent, while alerted to the performance problems of the other businesses. But when Eisner reminds readers of the top performance the company turned in throughout the 90s – when they had fewer "cylinders" – an astute investor may grow wary about the company's ability to manage this more complex enterprise. Even though such imaginative prose may distract us from the company's underlying problems, the passage leaves an impression. I'll remember that the company is more than just theme parks and animated movies.

Emotion and Stock Price

The distinction between creating emotion and describing emotion is important. Over the past three years, we found that the stock prices of companies whose CEOs create emotion in their letters increased, on average, by 11.9 percent. Conversely, the stock prices of companies whose CEOs do not create emotion in their shareholder letters increased by only 0.7 percent. Why this association?

Like it or not, the CEO sets and controls the emotional thermostat for the corporation. Managing the emotional life of a corporation has come to be regarded as one of the most important CEO abilities. John Kotter, the Harvard-based leadership expert, talked to me about the motivational power of CEOs in an interview in June 2000. He said:

The kind of leadership that really pays off today is one that helps people tap deep within themselves so they can find the energy to make and meet high standards. Then they can work hard without feeling like they're on a treadmill 18 hours a day. You need standards that connect to basic human values and help people create a sense of community. This holds them together against all the forces that drag us apart these days.[1]

If companies want to achieve extraordinary performance, their leaders need to be attuned to the hopes, aspirations, and desires of employees. They need to summon up the positive energy to overcome the fear, resentment, and self-defeating beliefs that inevitably hamper corporate progress, particularly in uncertain times. Athletes know the importance of aligning emotions with intention to perform at the top of their game. Companies that motivate employees and other stakeholders are more likely to perform better.

Other CEOs, like Eisner, are able to use dramatic imagery in their stories to create a lingering impression. But some stories do more. These stories create an emotional connection between the reader and the company. I call these, "You've Gotta Have Heart" stories.

Showing, Not Telling

One of my favorite "You've Gotta Have Heart" stories was included in Dominion Resources' 1998 shareholder letter. It takes the importance of customer service to a new level. Most companies list customer service in their litany of good corporate intentions. Not CEO Tom Capps. He describes a customer service experience in such vivid prose that you begin to feel you are a part of the experience:

Dominion Resources: Inundated With Cookies

In the last week of 1998, beginning the day before Christmas, severe ice storms tested the commitment, strength and ability of our front-line people. Ice broke down an uncountable number of trees, limbs and power lines. More than 440,000 homes and businesses lost power - thousands in need of individual attention. There is no computer known to man that is capable of pulling ice-laden debris off a downed power line, maneuvering a truck or a ladder to restore the wire and hooking it up safely, night or day. Every available Virginia Power crew worked a grueling schedule of restoration, beginning on Christmas Eve and continuing into the New Year.

"We've been inundated with cookies," reported Virginia Power's Joe Murphy, construction team leader, several days into the crisis. "Cookies by the pound, by the box, by the bag, by the sack,

satchel, plate, pitcher and handful. We've never been treated like this before. It's been amazing."

Combine great employees and great technology - and give your customers a reason to say "thanks." It's a strategy that works.

When I talked with a company spokesperson, I learned that I wasn't the only one paying attention to this story. One of the company's most important institutional investors called after he had read the annual report. He praised the letter and said that he particularly liked the Christmas cookie story, which nearly moved him to tears.

While both Eisner and Capps spin potent tales, in neither of their stories do they reveal their own emotions. CEOs who share their personal feelings are able to establish rapport with readers.

Up Close and Personal

Andrea Jung, the CEO of Avon, opened her shareholder letter with this personal statement (emphasis added):

As a business and as a brand, Avon has embarked on a journey of renewal and great opportunity. 2000 was an exciting year for us, and I feel privileged to be leading the company and serving you – its shareholders – as our performance and prospects have gathered momentum and strength.

Jung is one of the few CEOs who mentions the privilege of serving shareholders. When we totaled statements of hubris and humility in the 2000 shareholder letter survey, we found that hubris statements outscored humility by a two and a half to one margin.

In Alcoa's 2000 letter, CEO Alain Belda used emotional language to paint a portrait of his company's employees:

We value proactivity, flexibility, and a can-do attitude in our people, and we see them as the ultimate source of our company's power to create wealth.

Since employees in many cases are also shareholders, they make up a significant group of targeted readers. That's why I was astounded to find that 40 percent of the letters that I surveyed in

2000 failed to even acknowledge their employees. The excerpt from Alcoa's shareholder letter shows how a few well-chosen words can go a long way in affirming the connection between employees and corporate success.

Meg Whitman, eBay's CEO, describes the emotional experience eBay wants to create for its customers (emphasis added):

> *At eBay we do one thing. We work every day to be the world's largest and most compelling Internet commerce platform. To further that goal in 2000, our seasoned management team stayed focused on attracting more customers, expanding the goods traded on the site, making the user experience easier, safer, more fun and exciting, and spreading the eBay marketplace to more places around the world.*

She is one of a handful of CEOs who have started to portray the experience they expect customers to have in dealing with their companies in emotional terms.

Passion in Shareholder Letters

During CEO Jack Welch's 20-year reign, GE shareholders enjoyed an average annual 23 percent increase in their total return (stock price appreciation plus dividends). Few CEOs can boast about financial performance like this.

Fewer still write the kind of emotionally charged letters that Jack Welch published in GE's annual report. CEOs often tell me how much they admire and want to be like him. My guess is that they not only want to replicate GE's financial success under Welch's watch, but that they would also like to match his passion in their own business communications.

Welch, who knows the importance of language and open, "don't hold back" communication, valued my analysis of his shareholder letters. In an interview he told me he enjoyed writing his annual letter because it allowed him to crystallize his thoughts and "to give investors and employees a sense of what's in my heart and in my mind." When asked who he thought of when writing his letter, he didn't hesitate before answering, "Employees. They're our largest group of shareholders."

Each year GE employees are surveyed anonymously to learn whether they think the annual report accurately portrays the company they work for. Welch said, "The survey is another way for me to connect with employees. A lot of people write back to say the annual report did connect with them. Others tell us what isn't true, like those who don't feel as boundaryless as we'd like them to be. But generally we do pretty well."[2]

Throughout his career, Welch waged war against corporate bureaucracy. Look at the passion that flows in this passage from Welch's final shareholder letter in 2000:

GE: Annihilating Bureaucracy

We cultivate the hatred of bureaucracy in our Company and never for a moment hesitate to use that awful word "hate." Bureaucrats must be ridiculed and removed. They multiply in organizational layers and behind functional walls – which means that every day must be a battle to demolish this structure and keep the organization open, ventilated and free. Even if bureaucracy is largely exterminated, as it has been at GE, people need to be vigilant – even paranoid – because the allure of bureaucracy is part of human nature and hard to resist, and it can return in the blink of an eye. Bureaucracy frustrates people, distorts their priorities, limits their dreams and turns the face of the entire enterprise inward.

... It's about the four "E's" we've been using for years as a screen to pick our leaders. "Energy": to cope with the frenetic pace of change. "Energize": the ability to excite, to galvanize the organization and inspire it to action. "Edge": the self-confidence to make the tough calls, with "yeses" and "noes" – and very few "maybes." And "Execute": the ancient GE tradition of always delivering, never disappointing.

And it's about the four "types" that represent the way we evaluate and deal with our existing leaders. Type I: shares our values; makes the numbers – sky's the limit! Type II: doesn't share the values; doesn't make the numbers – gone. Type III: shares the values; misses the numbers – typically, another chance, or two.

None of these three are tough calls, but Type IV is the toughest call of all: the manager who doesn't share the values, but delivers the numbers; the "go-to" manager, the hammer, who delivers the bacon but does it on the backs of people, often "kissing up and kicking down" during the process. This type is the toughest to part with because organizations always want to deliver – it's in the blood – and to let someone go who gets the job done is yet another unnatural act. But we have to remove these Type IVs because they have the power, by themselves, to destroy the open, informal, trust-based culture we need to win today and tomorrow.

... In a digitized world, the internal workings of companies will be exposed to the world, and bureaucracies will be seen by all for what they are: slow, self-absorbed, customer insensitive – even silly.

Notice that he used the word "values" four times in this passage. In fact, the entire shareholder letter was devoted to a discussion of the importance of GE's values. Welch believes that his employees, most of whom are also shareholders, will read his letter. He uses the letter to reaffirm and recalibrate GE's moral and emotional compasses.

When CEOs begin to describe corporate values, their stories can start to sound like parables. In the next chapter I introduce stories to show that enduring truths are often associated with enduring businesses.

Chapter Thirteen

Enduring Truths and Businesses:
CEO and Corporate Values

VALUE. *Etymology: Middle English, from Middle French, from Vulgar Latin valuta, from feminine of valutus, p.part. of Latin valEre [to be worth, be strong] -- Date: 14th century*
  1. *a fair return or equivalent in goods, services, or money for something exchanged*
  2. *the monetary worth of something: marketable price*
  3. *relative worth, utility, or importance*
  4. *a numerical quantity that is assigned or is determined by calculation or measurement; precise signification*
  5. *the relative duration of a musical note*
  6. *relative lightness or darkness of a color; the relation of one part in a picture to another with respect to lightness and darkness*
  7. *something (as a principle or quality) intrinsically valuable or desirable*

  (Merriam-Webster Online Collegiate Dictionary)

Some CEO stories are more reflective than the ones described in the previous chapters. These rare shareholder letter stories reveal **"business truths and values."** Providing us with time-tested business wisdom, they resemble parables allowing readers to evaluate the character of the CEO and the company. We get to glimpse the presence or absence of moral strength that lies behind the CEO's promises.

Endurance in the Fast Food Industry
Robert J. Nugent, the CEO of Jack in the Box, describes the paradox of finding enduring business values in the fast food business. In his 2000 shareholder letter, he describes business basics that apply to any company or industry at any time:

Two Ways for Companies to Get Ahead

Very little in America looks much like it did 50 years ago. When the first Jack in the Box® restaurant opened in San Diego in 1951, the drive-thru concept was still a novelty, a harbinger of an emerging consumer culture that would come to place a sky-high premium on convenience, quality and good service. Half a century later, those three values still constitute the cornerstones of successful businesses in every industry.

The truth is, there have always been just two ways for companies to get ahead: One is to invent something wonderful that everyone needs but that's never existed before, thereby creating demand for a new product or service. The other is to take an existing product or service and do things a little bit better than your competition. We at Jack in the Box are synonymous with burgers, fries, sandwiches and shakes. But, though we'd like to be able to make the claim, we obviously didn't invent them. In the highly competitive business of fast food, where consumer loyalty in the form of repeat visits is a key measure of strength, our ongoing challenge in this, our 50th year in business, is to find new and better ways to deliver superior food to our guests. We made significant progress on that front this year, and, as they have for the past five years, our financial results reflect that progress.

Nugent reminds us that a company's financial results will improve when its strategy is built on these enduring truths – convenience, quality and good service – and when these truths are upheld in actions to customers.

Enduring Truths and Corporate Visions

The letters written by Lou Gerstner, IBM's former Chairman and CEO, are the most visionary in my survey. In his 2000 shareholder letter, he reflected on the dot.com crash and how it reaffirmed what is true and enduring in IBM's business.

IBM: e-Business, E-nough!

A year ago it looked as though Internet start-ups were taking over and traditional bricks-and-mortar enterprises had better jump with both feet into "e-tailing" or get steamrolled.

Well, as we all know today, it didn't happen. The crash brought out the usual pundits and weathervanes – the same ones who a year earlier had declared that dot-coms were taking over the world. Only now they were saying, "This e-business was mostly hype anyway. E-nough!"

Since, in many ways, IBM gave birth to all things "e" five years ago, I'd like to offer a perspective.

The collapse of the dot-coms was not a failure of e-business. It was the failure of an overly narrow approach to e-business. For all the proclamations we have been hearing about a "new economy," the problem with most dot-coms was that their business model – win customers through lower prices – wasn't anything new, not to mention transformative.

IBM has always said that e-business involves more than transforming one part of a company, such as selling directly over the Net. We said the real action, the real work – and the ultimate payoff – involved the transformation and the integration of the entire enterprise, from the customer all the way through the supply chain. Things have played out pretty much that way – and that may have been a bucket of cold water for some. For IBM, it was a tough but ultimately heartening reaffirmation of the strategic direction we set in place several years ago.

So, if there is a lesson to be extracted from the dot-com crash, it may be this: There is no short-cut to e-business. And if 2000 comes to be seen as a watershed (and I think it will), that will be because this was the year the world's established enterprises awoke to the true possibilities of e-business. I believe a broad consensus has emerged that e-business is just ... business, real business. And real business is serious work.

Gerstner expresses several enduring business truths. He reminds us that lower prices win customers, but that it doesn't guarantee enduring growth. He explains that the dot.com crash was not the failure of e-business, but the failure of a narrowly conceived business model. Finally, he states the obvious yet often forgotten fact: articulating business ideas is easy, executing them is tough and serious work.

The remainder of his letter describes just how IBM is capitalizing on its e-business strategy. These actions include rethinking and redoing the way that business functions are integrated all the way from customers to suppliers. Seen in this broader context, a reader gains appreciation for the durability IBM's strategy and execution.

Sticking with What You Understand: Circle of Competence

Here's what Buffett wrote in his 1999 shareholder letter about the importance of qualities that create an enduring competitive advantage. He cautions readers that the approach he follows is not necessarily one that is appreciated by those who look to stock market price as the sole measure of investing success. The importance of staying within his circle of competence is a principle followed by other successful investors like Peter Lynch:

We made few portfolio changes in 1999. As I mentioned earlier, several of the companies in which we have large investments had disappointing business results last year. Nevertheless, we believe these companies have important competitive advantages that will endure over time. This attribute, which makes for good long-term investment results, is one Charlie and I occasionally believe we can identify. More often, however, we can't – not at least with a high degree of conviction. This explains, by the way, why we don't own stocks of tech companies, even though we share the general view that our society will be transformed by their products and services. Our problem – which we can't solve by studying up – is that we have no insights into which participants in the tech field possess a truly durable competitive advantage.

Our lack of tech insights, we should add, does not distress us. After all, there are a great many business areas in which Charlie and I have no special capital-allocation expertise. For instance, we bring nothing to the table when it comes to evaluating patents, manufacturing processes or geological prospects. So we simply don't get into judgments in those fields.

If we have a strength, it is in recognizing when we are operating well within our circle of competence and when we are approaching the perimeter. Predicting the long-term economics of companies that operate in fast-changing industries is simply far beyond our perimeter. If others claim predictive skill in those industries – and seem to have their claims validated by the behavior of the stock market – we neither envy nor emulate them. Instead, we just stick with what we understand. If we stray, we will have done so inadvertently, not because we got restless and substituted hope for rationality. Fortunately, it's almost certain there will be opportunities from time to time for Berkshire to do well within the circle we've staked out.

Buffett reminds readers that his investing success is not innovative, nor original. It's simply the result of avoiding investments about which he knows little. Rather than choosing businesses whose values may be determined by the greater fool theory, he narrows his scope to focus on intrinsic value. This disciplined investing echoes what Lou Gerstner said earlier: a simple concept may be very difficult to execute.

Paper Values and Parables

Corporate values are different from business truths. They are deeper and more personal. Unfortunately, many CEOs describe their corporate values as if they were reminders on "sticky" notes. That was the Enron approach when it listed its corporate values in the 1999 shareholder letter:

Our values of communication, integrity, respect and excellence are equally applicable to our dealings with each other as with our customers and suppliers.

Does anyone need to be reminded of the hypocrisy of these statements? Our public cynicism is well-founded. Bull market prosperity shaped a cultural expectation that the fattest business prizes will go to those choosing to win at any cost. We've come to think about values like we think about marketing, advertising and staff support: costs to be cut when business fortunes change.

Imagine what children growing up during this time have learned. My daughter turned eight just about the time that dot.com stocks began to fall like soufflés. It wasn't long after her birthday that she asked me, "What's worse? Getting caught doing a bad thing or actually doing a bad thing?"

Do CEOs think that values are important? In January 2002, when Stephen Shepard, *BusinessWeek*'s Editor-in-Chief, asked the new CEO of GE, the largest company in the world, about what keeps him up at night, Jeffrey Immelt fired back: "Integrity." Only four months into his job, he explained, "I stay awake at night worrying that among the 300,000 people who work for GE, someone out there doesn't get it. What [we] can't live through is anybody who takes from the company or does something wrong in the community."[1] His former boss, Jack Welch, believed the CEO letter was a good way to recalibrate GE's moral compass. His last shareholder letter as CEO was all about GE's values.

But there's a difference between paper and real values. Paper values are found on fancy mission statement posters. Values become real when people act them out in space and time. Real values influence decisions and define the quality of corporate relationships. Real values can't be managed like cash flow and income statements.

Values in CEO Shareholder Letters

Maybe that is why so few companies disclose their corporate values in shareholder letters. Despite their obvious importance, they are mentioned by only 20 percent of the companies in my surveys from 1998-2000. In 2000, nine companies – GE, United UnitedHealth Group, DuPont, Pfizer, Kmart, AOL, Ford, McDonald's and Charles Schwab – acknowledged that values are important because they contribute to corporate success. The most commonly cited values were:

> Respect for people
> Inclusion and diversity
> Social responsibility
> Making a difference.

But few companies in my 2000 shareholder letter survey matched Citigroup's extended discussion on corporate values (emphasis added):

Diversity / Mutual Respect and Dignity

There should be no doubt that our people are the key to our success now and in the future, for our customers and our shareholders, and that they are our highest single priority. We seek to provide an environment – culture, job satisfaction, opportunity and compensation – that attracts and retains outstanding individuals all over the world. We embrace diversity, which is essential to our global orientation. And above all, we insist on a workplace founded on mutual respect, where everyone is treated with dignity.

Taking the Company Personally / Teamwork

We want every employee to be a shareholder and every employee to take the company personally – to care about each other, the quality of our products and services, and their value to our clients and shareholders. The people of Citigroup put customers first and are constantly striving to improve their performance. They are more interested in teamwork than in politics. And, they lead by example, giving credit to others for success and assuming personal responsibility for failure. Ours is a company for people who have a sense of urgency and excitement, who are candid, insightful and creative, and who thrive in an environment of change, challenge and competition. We value people who are committed to excellence in what they do, and we, in turn, are committed to creating the best possible environment for them to thrive in.

Moral and Ethical Conduct / Earning Trust

We aspire to be one of the great companies in the world, one that is completely client centered and provides unparalleled levels of customer service as a means of protecting and building our business franchise over time. We seek to be known as the company with the highest standards of moral and ethical conduct – working to earn client trust, day in and day out, through sound advice and shared wisdom.

Making a Difference, Pride, Tolerating Mistakes

We need to ensure that no matter how large we grow, our people feel that each and every one of them can make a difference. We want our people to share a sense of pride in Citigroup as well as in their particular business. We will continue to create a working environment where bureaucracy is discouraged, entrepreneurial thinking is fostered and where mistakes are tolerated, admitted to and addressed before they become real problems.

Community Service
We are also dedicated to community service. We take a leadership role in communities around the world in which we operate. We want every one of them to be better because we're there. We strive to build a company where the best people want to work and to be the first choice of where customers want to do business. That is our vision for Citigroup.

My company respects Citigroup for telling readers about its corporate values, but without linking them to specific examples and actions, they become just words on a piece of paper. They carry little weight.

The Values of Berkshire Hathaway
In contrast, Warren Buffett never uses the word "value" in his shareholder letters. Still, I came up with a list of twenty-three values that are described in the stories he tells in his 2000 shareholder letter. I call these:

Be Frugal and Multiply
Your Word is Your Bond
Trust Your People (Managers and Employees)
Don't Over Promise
Never Bet the Ranch
Admit Mistakes and Learn from Them
Expose Wrongdoing
Pride
Respect
Loyalty
Don't Discriminate on the Basis of Age
Pay for Performance
Safety First
Remember and Care for Your Family
Love What You Do
Know Your Strengths and Limitations

Give Credit When and Where It Is Due
Always Deliver Good Service and Low Prices
Never Sacrifice the Future for Short-Term Gain
Be Accountable and Speak Candidly with Your Partners
Be Fair to All Investors
Build a Sense of Community
Have Fun

Descriptions of two of these values from the 2000 shareholder letter – "Admit Mistakes" and "Your Word is Your Bond" – illustrate what makes these stand out from the discussion of values by other CEOs: They are personal and tied to specific actions:

Admit Mistakes
Last year I enthusiastically told you that we would step up our expenditures on advertising in 2000 and that the added dollars were the best investment that GEICO could make. I was wrong: The extra money we spent did not produce a commensurate increase in inquiries. Additionally, the percentage of inquiries that we converted into sales fell for the first time in many years. These negative developments combined to produce a sharp increase in our per-policy acquisition cost.

Agonizing over errors is a mistake. But acknowledging and analyzing them can be useful, though that practice is rare in corporate boardrooms. There, Charlie and I have almost never witnessed a candid post-mortem of a failed decision, particularly one involving an acquisition. A notable exception to this never-look-back approach is that of The Washington Post Company, which unfailingly and objectively reviews its acquisitions three years after they are made. Elsewhere, triumphs are trumpeted, but dumb decisions either get no follow-up or are rationalized.

Your Word is Your Bond
When a business masterpiece has been created by a lifetime or several lifetimes of unstinting care and exceptional talent, it should be important to the owner what corporation is entrusted to carry on its history. Charlie and I believe Berkshire provides an almost unique home. We take our obligations to the people who created a business very seriously, and Berkshire's ownership structure

ensures that we can fulfill our promises. When we tell John Justin that his business will remain headquartered in Fort Worth, or assure the Bridge family that its operation will not be merged with another jeweler, these sellers can take those promises to the bank.

In the first example, Buffett does what no other CEO has ever done in a shareholder letter: he admits he was wrong. In this example, he was wrong about spending more money to advertise GEICO. If you want to read more about what the company learned from this mistake, you can look on pages 10-12 of his 2000 shareholder letter.

Buffett's statements about his values are infused with his rich appreciation of human nature. In the second example, he describes the character of the people who run businesses he would like to buy. These executives don't run ordinary companies. Instead, they run "business masterpieces" created by their own inspiration and hard work. Buffett tells readers how he intends to honor these achievements – by making promises the sellers can take to the bank. In this example, readers can see how Berkshire's business success is achieved through motivating people rather than rearranging organization charts.

Capitalist Caper

Berkshire Hathaway's annual meeting offers concrete proof that Buffett and Munger live the financial golden rule of partnership and strive to be fair to all investors. While most corporations consider the annual shareholder meeting to be about as appealing as a root canal and hope for low attendance, Buffett believes the more the merrier. He calls his annual shareholder meeting a "Capitalist Caper." For the past seven years, thousands of Berkshire Hathaway shareholders have flocked to the company's annual meeting in Omaha.

In 2001, 15,000 shareholders descended on Nebraska's state capital. Buffett treats them all like VIPs. The company offers them the use of its own American Express travel agent. It gives them special discounts at hotels and at Berkshire-owned businesses, such as Dairy Queen, the Nebraska Furniture Mart and Borsheim's Jewelry store. Berkshire even hosts a cocktail party outside of Borsheim's the night before the meeting where the

"Berkies" (the name given to this group by Omaha natives) swig Cokes, shop for souvenirs (Borsheim's rings up a sizable percentage of its annual sales from this weekend shopping spree), swap investing stories, and await appearances by Buffett and Munger.

The annual meeting starts promptly the next morning at 8:30 a.m. with the showing of a "homemade" movie that is part *Monty Python* and part *Nightly News*. Afterwards, Buffett and Munger enter the stage to a standing ovation. They sit at a table behind cans of Coca-Cola and boxes of See's candies, which they munch on throughout the meeting.

Most corporations tightly control the agenda and investor participation at their annual meetings. Buffett and Munger answer questions for six hours and set only one ground rule: they will not talk about any company that they might buy or sell. Unlike many large open forum gatherings, there are surprisingly few frivolous or self-promoting questions or statements.

Tony Arrell, the Chairman of Burgundy Asset Management, a Toronto-based investment firm has attended 13 of the last Berkshire Hathaway annual meetings. His Burgundy Partners' Fund, based on Buffett's investment principles, has succeeded in returning 16.8 percent annualized to its investors since it began in 1993. When I ran into Arrell at intermission during the 2001 Berkshire meeting, he was beaming. Hoping to get his critical comments about the three hours of extensive Q & A, I asked, "What do you think?" Arrell smiled even more broadly and simply said, "It's like going to church."

Chapter Fourteen

Mae West and a Good CEO Letter:
Content, Efficiency and Stock Price

EFFICIENCY. *Etymology: Middle English, Old French, Latin, efficiens, efficient-, pr.part of efficere [to effect].*
1. *the quality or property of being efficient; the degree to which this quality is exercised*
2. *the ratio of the effective or useful output to the total input in any system; the ratio of the energy delivered by a machine to the energy supplied for its operation*
                    (American Heritage College Dictionary, Third Edition)

Mae West once said that it wasn't the number of men in her life, but the life in her men that was important. Similarly, I don't care about the number of words in a shareholder letter, I care about the life in the words. Most investors don't look at any words; they don't even read the letters. We know the common complaints:

The letters don't tell me anything.

It's a waste of my time to read them.

Reading them won't help me to become a better investor.

I've developed three ways to analyze and score shareholder letters to address these complaints. One measures the amount of content in a letter, another measures the **"letter's efficiency"** and a third correlates shareholder letter disclosure with stock price changes.

Measuring Content in Shareholder Letters

In the preceding chapters, you were introduced to 12 of the most important topics in my shareholder letter model. You need to remember these topics in order to measure the content value of a shareholder letter. Let's look at this excerpt from Buffett's 2000 shareholder letter about the acquisition of Benjamin Moore Paint:

In July, Bob Mundheim, a director of Benjamin Moore Paint, called to ask if Berkshire might be interested in acquiring it. I knew Bob from Salomon, where he was general counsel during some difficult times, and held him in very high regard. So my answer was "Tell me more."

In late August, Charlie and I met with Richard Roob and Yvan Dupuy, past and present CEOs of Benjamin Moore. We liked them; we liked the business; and we made a $1 billion cash offer on the spot. In October, their board approved the transaction, and we completed it in December. Benjamin Moore has been making paint for 117 years and has thousands of independent dealers that are a vital asset to its business. Make sure you specify our product for your next paint job.

How many shareholder letter topics can I identify in this passage? I find ten:

Berkshire Hathaway Letter Content	Language Works Topics	Points Scored
Has narrative elements that describe a business opportunity and grab the reader's interest.	*Story*	10
	Business Opportunity	10
Shows the Berkshire acquisition strategy of using trusted personal contacts to find outstanding businesses to buy.	*Strategic Sense*	10
	Emotion	10
	Values and Principles	10
Reports the amount of cash paid to acquire the business.	*Cash Flow*	10
Provides details about the physical assets and the company's reputation to show what's driving company profits.	*Profit Drivers*	10
Invites the reader to request Benjamin Moore paint when shopping in hopes of increasing company profits.	*Relationship with Reader/Investor*	10
	Business Opportunity	10

Respect for the reader's time and
intelligence by communicating   *Respect*   10
all this content in only 131 words.

It may be useful to compare shareholder letter topics to pins in a bowling alley. Whenever you can identify a topic, it's like knocking down a bowling pin. For simplicity's sake in this example, I assign a value of ten points for each pin that is knocked down. Thus, Buffett scores 100 Content points for the ten topics, or pins, that he knocks down in this passage – a "strike."

In contrast, here's an excerpt from Abbott Laboratories' 2000 shareholder letter, which reports on a recent acquisition the company made to expand its cardiovascular care business (emphasis added):

> *The foundation of this franchise is Perclose, Inc., which we acquired in late 1999. Perclose is a technology leader whose products offer both great patient benefit and high-growth potential in an attractive new market. The Perclose line of devices, which close arteries after interventional procedures with minimal recovery time, is used in the acute-care setting, where Abbott has outstanding presence. In its first year of ownership, Abbott grew Perclose sales by more than 60 percent.*

> *The acquisition of Perclose, however, was just the first step in a broader strategy. Abbott subsequently entered into agreements to develop and distribute embolic protection devices, which remove debris dislodged during cardiovascular procedures, before they can cause strokes and other organ damage. We have also forged alliances that will supply catheters to treat chronic total occlusions, which often otherwise result in by-pass surgery; and drug-coated stents, which will reduce the incidence of vessel restenosis. We now have a multi-faceted cardiovascular care business with breakthrough products that improve patient health and extend Abbott's reach into emerging, high-growth niche markets.*

When we apply the same analysis to this shareholder letter passage, we find that Abbott Labs has left more pins standing. It fails to connect with the reader either through dialogue or emotion; it has only a descriptive structure, not a narrative structure; and there is no mention of either cash flow or values. The letter describes the patient benefits in technical terms that are hard to understand: "We have also forged alliances that will supply catheters to treat chronic total occlusions, which often otherwise result in by-pass surgery; and drug-coated stents, which will reduce the incidence of vessel restenosis." We can't determine if this business opportunity is going to produce a steady flow of profits.

I can find only three of the 12 **LanguageWorks** topics:

Abbot Laboratories Letter Content	LanguageWorks Topics	Points Scored
Company acquired Perclose to build its acute- care business.	*Business Opportunity*	10
Sales grew 60 percent in this business.	*Financial Result*	10
Company wants to expand its cardiovascular business to improve patient health and grow in attractive markets.	*Strategic Sense*	10

Assigning our assumed ten points for each topic mentioned, we get only 30 Content points for this 175-word excerpt.

Measuring for Efficiency

Warren Buffett uses over 10,000 words to write Berkshire Hathaway's shareholder letter, almost four times the average number of words used in the letters in my survey. Do people refuse to read his letters because they are too long? No. People invariably say that Buffett's letter was "the longest and fastest read" of any shareholder letter. His letter is highly efficient.

Here's how I calculate Efficiency scores: I divide the Content points by the total number of words in the letter and multiply this result by 100. For example, dividing Abbott Lab's 30 Content points by 175 words, I get an Efficiency score of .17 or 17 points. When I divide Berkshire's 100 Content points by 134 words, I get an Efficiency score of .75 or 75 points. In other words, Buffett's writing is almost four and a half times more efficient than the writing by Abbott Labs.

Content Score Trends in 2000 Shareholder Letter Survey

The Content scores for the companies in my 2000 shareholder letter survey ranged from 1,336 points scored by top-ranked Wells Fargo to the 33 points scored by Nike's shareholder letter. The following companies ranked in the top and bottom 15 in Content for the year 2000 survey.

Content Score Rankings

Top 15 Scoring Companies			Bottom 15 Scoring Companies	
Rank	Company	Content Score	Company	Content Score
1	Wells Fargo & Company	1,336	Nike, Inc.	33
2	Ford Motor Company	1,075	Xerox Corporation	54
3	International Business Machines Corporation	1,071	Trump Hotels & Casino Resorts, Inc.	64
4	Continental Airlines, Inc.	994	Covanta Energy Corporation	97
5	Pfizer Inc.	800	MBNA Corporation	105
6	Burlington Northern Santa Fe Corporation	748	Dun & Bradstreet Inc.	106
7	Walt Disney Company	747	Williams Companies Inc.	111
8	Jack in the Box, Inc.	739	Metro-Goldwyn Mayer Studios, Inc.	133
9	General Electric Company	733	Revlon Consumer Products Corporation	137
10	Thermo Electron Corporation	695	Alltel Corporation	147
11	McDonald's Corporation	680	Dow Jones & Company, Inc.	153
12	American International Group, Inc.	659	The Great Atlantic & Pacific Tea Company	159
13	Marriott International Inc.	639	Burlington Resources Inc.	167
14	WellPoint Health Networks, Inc.	620	Humana Inc.	169
15	Bank of America Corporation	576	El Paso Corporation	177

Wells Fargo's letter was strong in describing the expectations of stakeholders. Nike's low ranking resulted from many confusing statements that reduced its overall score. (Berkshire Hathaway is not included in this survey because its Content scores, like the company's financial performance, are off the charts and would unfairly skew the overall results.)

Measuring Efficiency in CEO Shareholder Letters

Efficiency scores in my 2000 shareholder letter survey ranged from top-ranked Southwest Airlines, to lowest-ranked Nike. The following companies ranked among the top and bottom 15 companies in Efficiency for the year 2000 survey:

Efficiency Score Rankings

	Top 15 Scoring Companies			Bottom 15 Scoring Companies		
Rank	Company	# of Words	Eff. Score	Company	# of Words	Eff. Score
1	Southwest Airlines Co.	518	48.5	Nike, Inc.	1,287	2.6
2	Alcoa Inc.	793	48.3	Williams Companies Inc.	1,112	10.0
3	Walgreen Co.	1,131	42.0	Burlington Resources Inc.	1,182	14.1
4	Continental Airlines, Inc.	2,514	39.5	Covanta Energy Corporation	686	14.1
5	McDonald's Corporation	1,757	38.7	Trump Hotels & Casino Resorts, Inc.	436	14.7
6	Marriott International Inc.	1,695	37.7	First Union Corp.	2,090	14.9
7	MBNA Corporation	282	37.2	Procter & Gamble	1,459	14.9
8	Jack in the Box, Inc.	2,117	34.9	Abbott Laboratories	1,670	15.0
9	Cisco Systems, Inc.	1,405	34.3	NCR Corporation	1,978	15.4
10	Wells Fargo & Company	4,031	33.1	The ServiceMaster Company	2,435	15.9
11	Ford Motor Company	3,257	33.0	Qwest Communications International Inc.	1,207	16.0
12	Burlington Northern Santa Fe Corporation	2,279	32.8	Lucent Technologies Inc.	2,678	16.1
13	Humana Inc.	531	31.8	Motorola, Inc.	1,849	16.1
14	WellPoint Health Networks, Inc.	1,965	31.6	Walt Disney Company	4,440	16.8
15	Thermo Electron Corporation	2,206	31.0	Toys "R" Us, Inc.	1,810	16.9

The shortest letter in the survey was MBNA's 282 words. Walt Disney's CEO, Michael Eisner, used 4,440 words to write his letter. What's the optimum length of a shareholder letter? I tell CEOs the average length of top-ranked letters is between 2,500-3,000 words, while the lowest-ranked one average 800 words.

Measuring the Total Impact of a Shareholder Letter

Since content and efficiency are equally important qualities, I combine both scores and weight them to calculate a composite score measuring the shareholder letter's total impact. The top and bottom 15 ranked companies in Total Impact for the year 2000 survey:

Total Impact Score Rankings

	Top 15 Scoring Companies		Bottom 15 Scoring Companies	
Rank	Company	Total Impact Score	Company	Total Impact Score
1	Wells Fargo & Company	108.7	Nike, Inc.	4.4
2	Continental Airlines, Inc.	105.5	Trump Hotels & Casino Resorts, Inc.	13.2
3	Ford Motor Company	98.8	Xerox Corporation	13.6
4	McDonald's Corporation	95.4	Williams Companies Inc.	14.9
5	International Business Machines Corporation	95.2	Covanta Energy Corporation	15.8
6	Marriott International Inc.	92.3	Dun & Bradstreet Inc.	21.0
7	Jack in the Box, Inc.	92.2	Metro-Goldwyn Mayer Studios, Inc.	21.1
8	Alcoa Inc.	91.6	Revlon Consumer Products Corporation	21.3
9	Burlington Northern Santa Fe Corporation	89.6	Burlington Resources Inc.	21.7
10	Walgreen Co.	89.5	Dow Jones & Company, Inc.	23.5
11	Thermo Electron Corporation	85.9	El Paso Corporation	24.5
12	WellPoint Health Networks, Inc.	83.0	The Great Atlantic & Pacific Tea Company	25.0
13	Pfizer Inc.	79.9	Qwest Communications International Inc.	25.0
14	Cisco Systems, Inc.	79.7	Schlumberger Limited	25.0
15	Avon Products Inc.	78.3	Alltel Corporation	26.3

Company stock price changes are correlated with Total Impact scores in order to determine whether the quality of disclosure in a shareholder letter has any relationship with financial performance.

In the graph below, you can see the average percent stock price changes for top and bottom-ranked companies over three two-year periods. Each two-year period starts at the beginning of the year in which the shareholder letter is issued and ends two years later. For example, in the year 2000, the top 15 ranked companies increased an average of 7.4 percent from the beginning of 2000 to the beginning of 2002. Conversely, the prices of the 15 bottom-ranked companies declined 19.3 percent during this same two-year period:

Average Percent Two-Year Stock Price Change

Top and Bottom-Ranked Companies Scoring in LanguageWorks *for business*^{SM} Shareholder Letter Survey

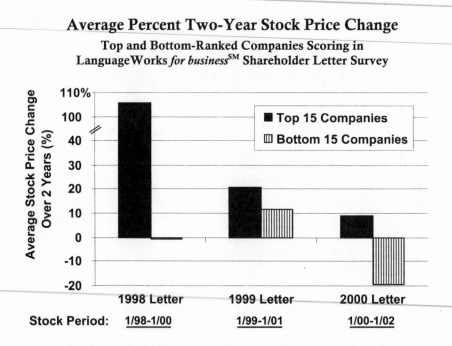

We can see that this positive correlation between shareholder letter disclosure and stock price changes has been sustained in each of our annual letter surveys from 1998 to 2000. The stock prices for the top-ranked companies have consistently outperformed the prices of the bottom-ranked companies in all three study periods. This was true during both the bull market in 1998 and the bear market which began in 2001.

But what about the stock prices of individual companies? For example, Ford Motor Company and McDonald's were both top-ranked in the 2000 language survey, but their stock prices declined during the period by 48 percent and 34 percent, respectively. Similarly, Nike and Burlington Resources were ranked in the bottom group, but they each gained 14 percent, respectively, during the study period.

These anomalies do not surprise me. Numerous factors determine the prices of stocks. It would be foolish to think that one factor – shareholder letter disclosure – could predict stock price performance with 100 percent accuracy. On the other hand, our trend analysis shows a surprisingly strong correlation between stock price performance and shareholder letter disclosure.

For example, in the 2000 survey 11 of the bottom-ranked companies posted price declines, but only five of the top-ranked companies posted declines. In 1999, five companies in each of the top and bottom-ranked groups posted declining stock prices. However, the stock price in the bottom-ranked groups declined on average by 54 percent, while the stock prices in the top-ranked group declined by only 30 percent. In 1998, only five companies in the top-ranked group posted price declines, while nine companies in the bottom-ranked group declined in price.

In other words, the correlation between stock price changes and the quality of shareholder letter disclosure has held up in each of the three periods studied. Companies that rank high in shareholder letter disclosure are more likely to show greater increases or smaller reductions in their stock prices than those that do not rank high.

What's the significance of this data? Common sense tells us that CEOs who are skilled communicators ought to enjoy a competitive advantage over those who are not. When leaders clearly communicate the company's principles and profit expectations to customers and investors, they build confidence in the company. When they walk their talk, they are more likely to extract better performance from employees. These CEOs can draw on "credibility currency" when times get tough.

Chapter Fifteen

CDO: Chief Disclosure Officer
The Shareholder Letter Scorecard

DISCLOSURE. *Etymology: from Middle English disclosen; Old French desclore, desclos- [to close]*
1. *the act or process of revealing or uncovering*
2. *something uncovered; a revelation*
                    (American Heritage College Dictionary, Third Edition)

"**Disclosure**" is a term frequently used in financial and legal circles to convey the importance of factual reporting. I have rarely seen the word used in the context of a "revelation" as noted above. I prefer this definition. It implies that disclosure can be surprising and highly significant.

The dot.com meltdown, the collapse of Enron, and the use of questionable accounting practices by other companies have all been unpleasant revelations. These events expose serious lapses in the oversight of our nation's financial and business institutions. The extent of Enron's alleged misrepresentations and its ability to hide them for so long has undermined our faith in accounting firms and in brokerage houses. It has even undermined our faith in the Securities and Exchange Commission (SEC), the government's financial watchdog.

Investors, governmental officials, and business leaders are demanding reforms. In March 2002, the SEC held hearings in New York City and invited distinguished financial experts, including Warren Buffett, to recommend ways to prevent future Enrons.

During the meeting, speakers advanced proposals to resolve potential conflicts of interest. They suggested splitting off equity research from investment banking at financial brokerage houses and separating audit services from consulting services at public accounting firms. They made other recommendations to strengthen the oversight functions of the existing agencies, such as the SEC, and to create new oversight bodies. Finally, they proposed new rules and stronger penalties for non-compliance.

Buffett was skeptical about adding more rules and bureaucracy to achieve greater accountability. He placed responsibility for high-quality, confidence-building disclosure squarely on the shoulders of the CEO. His proposal was simple: **that CEOs think of themselves as the company's Chief Disclosure Officer and write their own shareholder letters.** He said, "The CEOs attitude should be: 'What would I want to read if I were a shareholder?'"

Buffett hastened to add the importance of enlisting the services of a good editor. He frequently acknowledges the contributions of *Fortune Magazine's* Senior Editor, Carol Loomis, who edits his annual letter. Still, the CEO is singularly responsible for setting the company's disclosure standards.

Buffett went on to suggest that an organization, such as the Association of Investment Management and Research (AIMR), could be responsible for evaluating annual reports each year. The members of this body would determine whether a company's annual report comes across as a public relations report or a reliable disclosure document. If the organization found that a report had more fluff than substance, they would so inform the company. Would this have any impact? Buffett believed it would:

> *When we've withheld our vote on important matters, we hear from management. Companies get very interested in knowing who their owners are when that happens. With such a concentration of institutional ownership in this country, certainly, owners can get better reports if they want them.*[1]

Not only would institutional investors benefit from this proposal, so would individual investors.

CEO Disclosure and Individual Investors

The New York Stock Exchange states that one out of every two Americans now invests in the stock market. Electronic technology and financial products such as no-load mutual funds and 401(k) programs have turned investing into one of the nation's most popular pastimes. But individual investors can never enjoy the same access to top company management afforded to institutional investors. (Nor would this seem to be a good use of limited CEO time.)

For most individual investors, the annual shareholder letter and the annual shareholder meeting are the only ways they will ever get to visit with the CEO. Consequently, these investors have much to gain from improved shareholder letter disclosure. The stakes are high. If investors receive trustworthy disclosure in the shareholder letter, they will be better equipped to make their investment decisions.

Thanks to Arthur Levitt, the former SEC Commissioner, individual investors now have more access to real time corporate information than they did prior to the enactment of Regulation FD in 2001. This regulation puts teeth into the requirement that companies disclose fully and fairly to all investors, regardless of the number of owned shares. Even so, most individual investors believe that the odds in the game of investment are stacked against them. Not just Enron, but the failures of management oversight at Sunbeam, Cendant, Global Crossing and Qwest Communications have turned many into cynics.

The consequences of Enron's bankruptcy are still being absorbed by our financial system. One positive change is that we are finding much more detailed disclosure in this year's crop of 2001 annual reports. It is vital that these responsible efforts be recognized and continued.

The Shareholder Letter Scorecard

To further these disclosure advances, I have created a Shareholder Letter Scorecard. Now you can provide companies with important feedback. If you let CEOs know what you think about their ability to communicate meaningful information, they may even begin to write better shareholder letters.

A company that thanks you for your effort is a company worthy of your investment. A company that ignores your assessment may not represent a wise investment. The Shareholder Letter Subjects are described below:

1. CEO Voice: Personal and Authentic

When you finish reading the shareholder letter, do you feel like you had a meeting with the CEO? Do you feel as if the CEO is talking to you? Do you get a sense of the human face behind the CEO's public persona? Does the CEO suggest he or she is looking for a long or a short-term relationship?

2. Practicing the Financial Golden Rule

Is the CEO giving you information that he would expect to receive if he were the investor? Has the CEO addressed your general and specific questions and concerns about the company?

3. Detailed and Jargon Free Information

Is the CEO explaining complex topics in simple terms without "dumbing" down this information? Is the letter free of clichés and technical jargon? Are you getting relevant details that help you to make judgments about the profit and cash flow potential of the business and the company's intrinsic value?

4. Consistent and Realistic Information

Has the CEO provided historically consistent information, especially with regard to the company's earnings? Is the CEO explaining the company's goals and how the company intends to meet its goals? Does the CEO explain why the company's targets and other performance measures are realistic?

5. The Difference Between GAAP and Cash Earnings

Does the CEO letter reveal an understanding of the difference between the company's cash and accounting earnings? Can you find statements of earnings in the shareholder letter and easily locate this same number on the company's income statement in the annual report?

6. Balanced Strategic Sense

Does the CEO include a balanced picture of the execution of the company's strategy and its results? Are you learning about the year's business failures as well as the successes? How is the CEO addressing the company's problems?

7. CEO Values

Is the CEO describing his or her values and are these related to specific events in the company? Do you gain more understanding about how the CEO and his or her company practice these values in relation to their corporate stakeholders: employees, customers, investors, suppliers and others?

After reviewing these subjects, pick up your pencil and begin to analyze the shareholder letter. Read between the lines. Look for attitude. Then fill in the Scorecard on the following page. Send it to the CEO. Or go to my website (www.andbeyondcom.com.) and download this Scorecard. Fill in your grades and e-mail it to the company. If you send it to us, we will forward it to the company.

Warren Buffett likes to point out that managements get the investors they deserve. Similarly, investors get the managements they deserve. Here's your chance to let your voice be heard. Concerned that it won't make a difference? Read this story sent to me by a friend:

> *Driving home from work the other day, I stopped to watch a Little League baseball game. As I sat down behind the dugout, I asked one of the boys what the score was. "We're behind 14 to nothing," he answered, smiling. "Really?" I said, "I have to say, you don't look very discouraged."*
>
> *"Discouraged?" the boy asked with a puzzled look. "Why should we be discouraged? We haven't been up to bat yet."*

LanguageWorks *for business*^{SM}

Shareholder Letter Scorecard

Company: _____

"A"	"B"	"C"	"D"	"F"
4 pts I strongly agree	**3 pts** I somewhat agree	**2 pt** I somewhat disagree	**1 pts** I strongly disagree	**0 pts** No Opinion

	Grade / Score
CEO Voice After reading the letter, I feel like I just had a meeting with the CEO.	_____
Practicing the Financial Golden Rule The CEO is giving me information the way that he or she would want if our roles were reversed.	_____
Detailed, Clear and Jargon-Free Information The CEO is clearly explaining complex business topics in language that is free of clichés and technical jargon.	_____
Clear, Consistent Realistic Information The CEO is providing consistent earnings results and setting reasonable business goals and expectations.	_____
GAAP and Cash The CEO explains and reconciles the gap between cash and accounting earnings.	_____
Balanced Strategic Sense The CEO describes the successes and failures in the company's strategy and discloses how the company is addressing its problems.	_____
CEO Values The CEO describes the company's principles and values and shows how they influence corporate decisions, actions and stakeholder relationships.	_____
CEO SCORE	_____

An Interview with Warren E. Buffett

Chairman and CEO, Berkshire Hathaway Inc.

June 4, 2001

Do CEOs Write Their Own Letters?

LJR: *If you were deciding to invest in a company, how would the CEO letter influence your decision and what would you look for?*

Buffett: It's a significant factor, although not the only factor. First I decide whether he or she wrote it or whether somebody in the PR department or an outside consultant wrote it. I can usually tell.

I grade them higher if I feel they wrote it. What I look for is someone that is talking to me frankly and honestly about the business, the way a partner would. If they're talking to me as a partner would, that's a significant plus. If they aren't, it's a significant minus.

LJR: *What are the signals that a PR firm wrote it?*

Buffett: It's like the Supreme Court said about pornography. You know it when you see it.

LJR: *Tell me about your creative process.*

Buffett: I just sit down in late November and I dictate the whole thing very quickly. It reads like a bunch of garbage when I get it back, but at least it gets my train of thought in a logical formation. Then I clean it up, and I clean it up, and I clean it up. After that I send it to Carol Loomis for editing. When she sends it back, I almost have to start all over again.

The last five percent of it takes about 95 percent of the time. That's the way it works. Once I sat next to Agnes Nixon who created "All My Children" and other soap operas. I met her at the

Calgary Olympics. She studied under some famous writing professor at Northwestern who told her, there is always the "right" word. I believe that. Until you get the right word, forget about the rest. You've got to have the right word.

If you can't explain an idea, you haven't got your own thinking correct yet. So you're searching to get it just right. This is a very tough process. In my case, I just try to get an even flow of ideas the first or second time around. I don't try to make sentences, or paragraphs, or even whole sections read well or correctly at the start. I want it to sound as if I was talking to my sisters about what happened in the business.

LJR: *How do you know when the letter is done?*

Buffett: It's done when they tell me I have to give it to the printer! We file our 10K by March. Because of our annual meeting schedule, we have to hand it to the printer the first day or two of March. Some parts of the letter involving the final numbers get entered a couple of days later. We're not geared up to either print or mail as fast as some others. From the time I have it at the printer, it takes about ten days before it gets back ready to be mailed. But it's done on the last day I can get it done.

LJR: *So if you had more time, you'd spend it?*

Buffett: I'd probably fool around with it. It's really done by then, but I can't resist playing around with it a little bit. It's just the nature of it.

LJR: *You seem to have fun writing it.*

Buffett: Yes, I have fun. But it's painful; writing is painful. In the end, I'm glad that I spent the time I did. There are a lot of things that I want to cover in the way of business principles, as well as the specific activities of Berkshire.

LJR: *But what makes it painful?*

Buffett: Writing is just hard work. It's very discouraging to spend thirty minutes on one paragraph and feel that you still haven't quite got it right. I've done that in order to say exactly what I want so that a good many of the 300,000 people who read it will understand what I'm writing about. Getting across fairly complex ideas is tough work.

LJR: *Is that why you think a lot of CEOs don't do it?*

Buffett: They're used to turning things over to a staff. I'm used to doing everything around here myself. Also, I think many of them don't think that well about their businesses. This would get exposed if they tried to write it themselves.

LJR: *You are anticipating my next question: Do investors gain if CEOs spend the amount of time you do writing?*

Buffett: Yes. If the CEO doesn't write it, it's a black mark against them for one reason – they may not know their business very well. Plenty of CEOs don't understand their business as well as a lot of people outside their business, or even the people who work for them. They don't want to be seen as they really are.

It would be like a guy talking about golf, but never playing, and saying how great a golfer he was, or having somebody else go around saying how great he is. If CEOs don't talk to me directly, I'm suspect. Why should I give them my money?

Berkshire itself owns subsidiaries. I certainly don't want the person who runs See's Candies, or *The Buffalo News* for Berkshire, to hire some public relations firm to tell me what's going on. Why should our owners feel any differently in relation to me, who they've hired to run Berkshire?

LJR: *You're touching on an important idea – the notion that writing isn't just about writing, but is about living. What you're saying is if a CEO writes very clearly about what he's done and intends to do, he actually has to do it.*

Buffett: Yes, that's right. They have to do it. Knowing that a good reporter is going to report on you may inspire you to do a little bit better. When writing a shareholder letter, that good reporter should be the CEO himself.

The name of the document is "Annual Report." It's not the annual sales promotion piece or the annual puff piece. It's not a picture book about the company. It's the annual report. And that's what it's supposed to be, a report.

LJR: So you need a lot of confidence to put out a report that has no glossy pictures in it.

Buffett: The truth is there are no pictures that would aid in understanding Berkshire. But 10,000 words will if they're carefully chosen. I want our partners to understand what we're all about. I want them to understand how I measure our success, what our policies are, why those are our policies, and things we don't do. They should hear it and I should be able to explain it. If I can't explain it, then maybe I haven't thought it out very well.

LJR: Was it tough writing last year's letter when your stock was trading around $40,000 down from $70,000?

Buffett: No, the effort is just about the same. I enjoy writing them. For example, if we have a lousy year, I sort of enjoy reporting the facts about it. That's a real test!

LJR: Is it true that you think about members of your family when you are writing your shareholder letter?

Buffett: I think of my two sisters, because they're both very smart and they both have all their money in Berkshire. They're not business or investment experts, but they can understand things. I should be able to explain any business or investment to them, even though they are not necessarily familiar with all the jargon. That's who I'm writing for.

LJR: Do they get to see it before it is printed?

Buffett: No. I just imagine them. In my mind, the letter starts out "Dear Bertie and Doris." Then I go from there, and I take away the "Bertie and Doris" and put in "To the Shareholders of Berkshire Hathaway."

But that's my mindset when I write. I think of my silent business partners. If you're running a business for somebody, whether its a service station or McDonald's stand or whatever it is, you should imagine you are writing to your silent partner who put up the money.

LJR: *This partnership idea is very important to you and shows through in your letters.*

Buffett: Yes, it is fundamental. If you look at our economic ground rules at the back of the report, it's the first one: though our form is corporate, our attitude is partnership.

LJR: *Why don't other companies write Owner's Manuals?*

Buffett: Part of the problem is they don't have principles. I don't mean that they're unprincipled people, but they don't have principles about shareholders. They'd have a hard time writing it.

LJR: *But it would force them to think that through.*

Buffett: Absolutely. But they're doing fine without it. In the end, it doesn't make them wealthier or anything. It's like Charlie says – the one thing we've got is the fiduciary gene. We don't have a Mother Teresa gene, however. Or at least it's not that strong.

LJR: *Where do your best ideas come from? Do you just scribble stuff during the year and say you think you want to write about this?*

Buffett: Sometimes I do that, yes. If I think I might forget about it, I'll scribble it down. All kinds of things come along in a year. I always get enough material for a 10,000 word report.

In fact, that's part of the problem. Early on, I asked Meg Greenfield, a wonderful Editor for the *Washington Post* to look at one of my letters. She said, "Warren, you don't have to tell all you know in one piece." I still remember her advice. She sensed that I was going on too long. If somebody has five or ten thousand dollars invested with you, they ought to be interested enough to read a reasonable amount, as long as you're making it interesting to them. It's a significant commitment of their time.

LJR: *The problem is so many people don't make it interesting. They've kind of trained people not to read their shareholder letters.*

Buffett: You've got to tell stories and that sort of thing.

LJR: *Did you have any idea when you started writing your letters that they would become such an important part of the Berkshire Hathaway legacy?*

Buffett: It really started back when I was 25 years old, in 1956. That was the year I wrote my first partnership letter. The partners then were all related to me. I felt I owed them that. I never told them what securities I bought, even back then. But I wanted to explain to them how we operated, the rationale, what I thought, and all of that. I still have all the reports back to that 1956 partnership which preceded Berkshire. It's evolved since then. Berkshire has become a more complicated enterprise. There's more to explain now.

LJR: *Do you get fan mail from people about your letters?*

Buffett: I hear about it all over. When I speak at business schools, students will quote from reports written twenty years ago. That's rewarding. Sure, I get a lot of fan mail. Actually, I like that. I wouldn't be human if I didn't.

Endnotes:

Chapter 1

1. Andrew Kilpatrick, *Of Permanent Value: The Story of Warren Buffett*, (Birmingham, AL: Andy Kilpatrick Publishing Empire, 2000) 3.

2. Warren Buffett: Telephone Interview. 21 Jan. 2002.

3. Warren Buffett: Telephone Interview. 21 Jan. 2002.

4. Warren Buffett: Telephone Interview. 21 Jan. 2002.

5. New York Stock Exchange, Inc. *The 2000 Fact Book*. New York, NY: NYSE, Inc., 2000.

6. Warren Buffett: Telephone Interview. 4 June 2001.

7. "Executive Compensation Scoreboard." *BusinessWeek* Apr. 15, 2002.

8. Berkshire Hathaway Inc. *2000 Annual Report*. Omaha, NB: Berkshire Hathaway Inc., 2000.

9. "Berkshire Hathaway's Warren Buffett and Charlie Munger." *Outstanding Investor Digest* 24 Sep. 1998: 55.

10. Sarah Anderson, et al., "Executive Excess 2001, Eighth Annual CEO Compensation Survey." Institute for Policy Studies; United for a Fair Economy. Aug. 2001.

11. Sarah Anderson, et al., "Executive Excess 2000, Seventh Annual CEO Compensation Survey." Institute for Policy Studies; United for a Fair Economy. Aug. 2000.

12. Warren Buffett: Telephone Interview. 4 June 2001.

13. "Measures That Matter." The Ernst & Young Center for Business Innovation, Cambridge, MA 1987.

14. Warren Buffett: Telephone Interview. 4 June 2001.

Chapter 2

1. "How to Read Your Annual Report." Host Daryn Kagan. *In The Money 101*. CNN 18 Jan. 2000.

2. Warren Buffett: Telephone Interview. 4 June 2001.

3. **LanguageWorks *for business*^{SM}**. New York, NY: andBEYOND Communications Inc., 2002.

4. Warren Buffett: Telephone Interview. 4 June 2001.

5. Burlington Resources Inc. *2000 Annual Report*. Houston, TX: Burlington Resources Inc., 2000.

6. "Shareholder Letter Process Survey Report." UtiliVentures Inc., New York, NY, 1999.

7. *The Wizard of Oz*. Dir. Victor Fleming. Metro-Goldwyn-Mayer Studios, Inc., 1939.

Chapter 3

1. Berkshire Hathaway Inc. *1983 Annual Report*. Omaha, NB: Berkshire Hathaway Inc., 1983.

2. Warren Buffett: Telephone Interview. 4 June 2001.

3. Selena Maranjian, "Buffett and Munger Answer Questions in Omaha at 2000 Annual Meeting." 4 May 2002
< http://www.fool.com/specials/2000/sp000504a.htm>

Chapter 7

1. "Italian Renaissance: Birth of Double Entry." Association of Chartered Accountants in the U.S. 2002
<http://www.acaus.org/history/hs_pac.html>

Chapter 12

1. L.J. Rittenhouse. "Culture, Dreams and Shareholder Value." *Shareholder Value Magazine* Jan./Feb. 2001: 46.

2. Jack Welch: Telephone Interview. 21 July 2001.

Chapter 13

1. "Captains of Industry Series: A Talk with Jeff Immelt." 28 Jan. 2002
<http://www.businessweek.com/magazine/content/02_04/b3767079.htm>

Chapter 15

1. U.S. Securities and Exchange Commission, "Roundtable Discussion on Financial Disclosure and Auditor Oversight." 4 Mar. 2002
<http://www.sec.gov/spotlight/roundtables/accountround030402.htm>